THE LETTERS OF CENTINEL

"For remember, of all *possible* evils, *despotism* is the *worst* and the most to be dreaded."

THE LETTERS OF CENTINEL:
Attacks on the U.S. Constitution 1787-1788

Samuel Bryan

Edited and Introduced by Warren Hope

Fifth Season
P R E S S
Ardmore, PA

Library of Congress Catalog Number: 98-74072
ISBN: 1-892355-01-9

Annotated Edition, November 1998
Printed in the U.S.A.

Contents

Introduction:
A Forgotten Classic

The twenty-four letters Samuel Bryan wrote and published under the pen name "Centinel" during the debate over what became the Constitution of the United States are classics of American political writing that remain all but unknown. The reasons for the thick silence that settled on these letters are not far to seek.

First, Bryan opposed ratification of the Constitution. If Americans are often sympathetic to underdogs, they have little patience with devotees of lost causes.

Second, Bryan makes short work of some of our most cherished political myths. He calls the framers and advocates of the Constitution "conspirators" and makes a strong case for the accuracy of the label. He forcibly reminds us of what too many of us too often forget: the Constitution originally included no Bill of Rights and one would not have been added to it without the raised voices of Bryan and others like him. He shows that the governmental "checks and balances" in which we take so much pride provide an exceedingly thin reed on which to depend for the preservation of liberty. In short, he is a democrat—with a small "d"—appalled by the ghastly sight of America's hard-won experiment in democratic republicanism heading south as early as 1787.

Third, Bryan's language is clear and impassioned, the reflection of a mind guided by principles in its struggle with actualities. It has a rude, shocking quality now that we have become mentally numb from the perpetual murmurings of political somnambulists, the reflection of minds guided by indifference in their struggles with inanities. One historian describes the *Letters of Centinel* as "scathing," but he does not seem to understand why they strike him as scathing. Bryan meant what he said: "...of all *possible* evils, that of *despotism* is the *worst* and the most to be dreaded." How can these letters appear to be anything other than scathing when they are read by people who can think of fifty-seven varieties of evils far worse and more to be dreaded than despotism—inconvenience, discomfort, insecurity, anything less than 128 channels reachable by a flick of the remote, and so on?

In fact, the reasons for the silence that surrounds these letters are the very characteristics that make them American classics. As the historian Charles Beard recognized in 1913, the *Letters of Centinel*

1

demand comparison with that very different and very well-known classic of American political writing, *The Federalist Papers*.

"Publius," the pen name used by Alexander Hamilton, John Jay, and James Madison to advocate ratification of the proposed Constitution in *The Federalist Papers*, never refers to "Centinel" by name, but it is clear that they are at times responding to him. "Centinel" refers to "Publius" once, but in memorable language that exposes the most serious flaw in the arguments of "Publius":

> The other specter that has been raised to terrify and alarm the people out of the exercise of their judgment on the great occasion, is the dread of our splitting into separate confederacies or republics, that might become rival powers and consequently liable to mutual wars from the usual motives of contention... This hobglobin appears to have sprung from the deranged brain of *Publius*, a New York writer, who, mistaking sound for argument, has with Herculean labor accumulated myriads of unmeaning sentences, and *mechanically* endeavored to force conviction by a torrent of misplaced words.

If despotism is the worst of all possible evils for "Centinel," liberty is the greatest of all possible blessings. For "Publius," on the other hand, political instability is the worst of all possible evils and a strong national government, marked by "efficiency and vigor," is the greatest of all possible blessings. Hamilton, writing as "Publius," all but says as much in the first and last paragraphs of *The Federalist Papers*. Federalist No. 1 opens with these words:

> After an unequivocal experience of the inefficiency of the subsisting Federal Government, you are called upon to deliberate on a new Constitution for the United States of America. The subject speaks its own importance; comprehending in its consequences, nothing less than the existence of the Union, the safety and welfare of the parts of which it is composed, the fate of an empire, in many respects the most interesting in the world.

Federalist No. 85 closes the series of papers this way:

> A Nation without a National Government is, in my view, an awful spectacle. The establishment of a constitution, in time of profound peace, by the voluntary consent of a whole people, is a Prodigy, to the completion of which I look forward with trembling anxiety. I can reconcile it to no rules of prudence to let go the hold we now

Introduction

have, in so arduous an enterprise, upon seven out of the thirteen states; and after having passed over so considerable a part of the ground to recommence the course. I dread the more the consequences of new attempts, because I know that Powerful Individuals, in this and in other states, are enemies to a general national government, in every possible shape.

The positions of "Centinel" and "Publius" on every particular issue derive from their competing sets of principles. "Centinel" favors a Bill of Rights. "Publius" opposes one. "Centinel" favors a simple governmental structure answerable directly to the people. "Publius" favors a complex form of government with "checks and balances" to protect the wishes of the few from the whims of the many. "Centinel" publicly blushes with shame that the "odious traffic in the human species," the importation of slaves, is to continue for twenty-one years under the proposed Constitution. "Publius" considers the same provision "a great point gained in favor of humanity." "Centinel" denounces the desire for a standing army in time of peace. "Publius" applauds it.

Centinel's letters do not only differ from *The Federalist Papers* in their guiding principles and in the particular positions they advocate, but also in one other way: the *Letters of Centinel* have an integrity that cannot be claimed for *The Federalist Papers*.

It is not simply that "Publius" was the pen name of three men, a little committee. Some scholars suggest that Samuel Bryan's more famous father, George Bryan, best remembered as the author of the first law to provide for the abolition of slavery in the United States, and Eleazer Oswald, the publisher of *The Independent Gazetteer*, the Philadelphia newspaper where the *Letters of Centinel* first appeared, authored portions of the letters signed "Centinel." The integrity I mean comes from the fact that Samuel Bryan consistently took the same positions he held as "Centinel" both privately and publicly, before and after the debate over the Constitution. The same certainly cannot be said of Alexander Hamilton, the driving force behind *The Federalist Papers*.

As early as May, 1785, Samuel Bryan wrote in a private letter to his father describing popular dissatisfaction with the Articles of Confederation as a "general disposition in people to vest congress with efficient powers for the regulation of commerce." In Centinel No. 4, he describes the need to strengthen the federal government under the Articles of Confederation this way:

> A transfer to Congress of the power of imposing imposts on commerce and the unlimited regulation of trade, I believe is all that is wanting to render America as prosperous as it is in the power of any form of government to render her; this properly understood would meet the views of all the honest and well-meaning.

In December, 1789, Bryan wrote to Aedanus Burke of South Carolina in response to questions put by Burke as a way to gather information for a history of the ratification of the Constitution:

> The Writer of this had confined his Views of Alteration to be made in the old Confederation to a mere Enlargement of the Powers of Congress, particularly as to maritime Affairs. He thinks the Experiment ought at least to have been tried, whether we could not have succeeded under a Confederation of independent States, before we proceeded to consolidate all power in one general Government.

This consistency, integrity, compares very favorably with the positions taken privately and publicly by Alexander Hamilton. We now know from Madison's *Notes of Debates in the Federal Convention of 1787* that Hamilton was at heart a monarchist who felt compelled to support a republic because the poor befuddled masses of Americans would not tolerate a monarchy so soon after the Revolution. "In his private opinion," Madison tells us Hamilton announced to the Convention, "he had no scruple in declaring, supported as he was by the opinions of so many of the wise & good, that the British Govt was the best in the world: and that he doubted much whether any thing short of it would do in America." Hamilton publicly supported the proposed Constitution because it went as far as was then possible in undoing the American Revolution. Bryan opposed the proposed Constitution in an effort to strengthen the federal government while preserving as much as was then possible of the gains in liberty won by the Revolution.

The *Letters of Centinel* are part of a submerged tradition in American political thought that is more desperately needed now that the rulers of our televisionary Republic have become accustomed to playing imperial games than it was in the days when the imperial dreams

Introduction

of America's first rulers were new. It is a tradition that stretches from Thomas Paine, the man who preceded Samuel Bryan as secretary to Pennsylvania's revolutionary government, through David Graham Phillips, the muckraking author who instigated the popular election of senators by writing *The Treason of the Senate*, to more recent lone voices crying in the American wilderness. It is a tradition devoted to a cause that is never totally lost and never permanently won, the cause of republican government as described by Samuel Bryan in the first of his letters:

> A republican, or free government, can only exist where the body of the people are virtuous, and where property is pretty equally divided. In such a government the people are the sovereign and their sense or opinion is the criterion of every public measure; for when this ceases to be the case, the nature of the government is changed, and an aristocracy, monarchy or despotism will rise on its ruin.

Warren Hope

MR. OSWALD: *As the Independent Gazetteer seems free for the discussion of all public matters, I expect you will give the following a place in your next.*

To the FREEMEN of PENNSYLVANIA *Friends, Countrymen and Fellow Citizens.*

Permit one of yourselves to put you in mind of certain *liberties* and *privileges* secured to you by the constitution of this commonwealth, and to beg your serious attention to his uninterested opinion upon the plan of federal government submitted to your consideration, before you surrender these great and valuable privileges up forever. Your present frame of government secures to you a right to hold yourselves, houses, papers and possessions free from search and seizure, and therefore warrants granted without oaths or affirmations first made, affording sufficient foundations for them, whereby any officer or messenger may be commanded or required to search your houses or seize your persons or property not particularly described in such warrant, shall not be granted. Your constitution further provides "that in controversies respecting property, and in suits between man and man, the parties have a right *to trial by jury, which ought to be held sacred.*" It also provides and declares, *"that the people have a right of* FREEDOM OF SPEECH, *and of* WRITING *and* PUBLISHING *their sentiments,* therefore THE FREEDOM OF THE PRESS OUGHT NOT TO BE RESTRAINED." The constitution of Pennsylvania is *yet* in existence, *as yet* you have the right to *freedom of speech,* and of *publishing your sentiments.* How long those rights will appertain to you, you yourselves are called upon to say; whether your *houses* shall continue to be your *castles,* whether your *papers,* your *persons* and your *property,* are to be held sacred and free from *general warrants,* you are now to determine. Whether the *trial by jury* is to continue as your birth-right, the freemen of Pennsylvania, nay, of all America, are now called upon to declare.

Without presuming upon my own judgment, I cannot think it an unwarrantable presumption to offer my private opinion, and call upon others for theirs; and if I use my pen with the boldness of a freeman, it is because I know that *the liberty of the press yet remains unviolated and juries yet are judges.*

The late Convention have submitted to your consideration a plan of a new federal government. The subject is highly interesting to your future welfare. Whether it be calculated to promote the great ends of civil society, viz., the happiness and prosperity of the community, it behoves you well to consider, uninfluenced by the authority of names.[1] Instead of that frenzy of enthusiasm, that has actuated the citizens of Philadelphia, in their approbation of the proposed plan, before it was possible that it could be the result of a rational investigation into its principles, it ought to be dispassionately and deliberately examined on its own intrinsic merit, the only criterion of your patronage. If ever free and unbiased discussion was proper or necessary, it is on such an occasion. All the blessings of liberty and the dearest privileges of freemen are now at stake and dependent on your present conduct. Those who are competent to the task of developing the principles of government, ought to be encouraged to come forward, and thereby the better enable the people to make a proper judgment; for the science of government is so abstruse, that few are able to judge for themselves. Without such assistance the people are too apt to yield an implicit assent to the opinions of those characters whose abilities are held in the highest esteem, and to those in whose integrity and patriotism they can confide; not considering that the love of domination is generally in proportion to talents, abilities and superior requirements, and that the men of the greatest purity of intention may be made instruments of despotism in the hands of the *artful and designing*. If it were not for the stability and attachment which time and habit gives to forms of government, it would be in the power of the enlightened and aspiring few, if they should combine, at any time to destroy the best establishments, and even make the people the instruments of their own subjugation.

The late revolution having effaced in a great measure all former habits, and the present institutions are so recent, that there exists not that great reluctance to innovation, so remarkable in old communities, and which accords with reason, for the most comprehensive mind cannot foresee the full operation of material changes on civil polity; it is the genius of the common law to resist innovation.

The wealthy and ambitious, who in every community think they have a right to lord it over their fellow creatures, have availed themselves very successfully of this favorable disposition; for the people thus unsettled in their sentiments, have been prepared to accede to any extreme of government. All the distresses and difficulties they experience, proceeding from various causes, have been ascribed to the impotency of the present confederation, and thence they have been led to expect full relief from the adoption of the proposed system of government; and in the other event, immediately ruin and annihilation as a nation. These characters flatter themselves that they have lulled all distrust and jealousy of their new plan, by gaining the concurrence of the two men in whom America has the highest confidence, and now triumphantly exult in the completion of their long mediated schemes of power and aggrandizement.[2] I would be very far from insinuating that the two illustrious personages alluded to, have not the welfare of their country at heart; but that the unsuspecting goodness and zeal of the one has been imposed on, in a subject of which he must be necessarily inexperienced, from his other arduous engagements; and that the weakness and indecision attendant on old age, has been practiced on in the other.

I am fearful that the principles of government inculcated in Mr. Adams' treatise, and enforced in the numerous essays and paragraphs in the newspapers, have misled some well designing members of the late Convention. But it will appear in the sequel, that the construction of the proposed plan of government is infinitely more extravagant.

I have been anxiously expecting that some enlightened patriot would, ere this, have taken up the pen to expose the futility, and counteract the baneful tendency of such principles. Mr. Adams' *sine qua non* of a good government is three balancing powers; whose repelling qualities are to produce an equilibrium of interests, and thereby promote the happiness of the whole community. He asserts that the administrators of every government, will ever be actuated by views of private interest and ambition, to the prejudice of the public good; that therefore the only effectual method to secure the rights of the people and promote their welfare, is to create an opposition of interests between the members of two distinct bodies, in the exercise of the powers of government, and balanced by those of a third. This hypothesis supposes human wisdom competent to the task of instituting three co-equal orders in government, and a corresponding weight in the community to enable them respectively to exercise their several parts, and whose views and interests should be so distinct as to prevent a coalition of any two of them for the destruction of the third.[3] Mr. Adams, although he has traced the constitution of every form of government that ever existed, as far as history affords materials, has not been able to adduce a single instance of such a government; he indeed says that the British constitution is such in theory, but this is rather a confirmation that his principles are chimerical and not to be reduced to practice. If such an organization of power were practicable, how long would it continue? Not a day—for there is so great a disparity in the talents, wisdom and industry of mankind, that the scale would presently preponderate to one or the other body, and with every accession of power the means of further increase would be greatly extended. The state of society in England is much more favorable to such a scheme of government than that of America. There they have a powerful hereditary nobility, and real distinctions of rank and interests; but even there, for want of that perfect equality of power and distinction of interests in the three orders of government, they exist but in name; the only operative and efficient check upon the conduct of administration, is the sense of the people at large.[4]

Suppose a government could be formed and supported on such principles, would it answer the great purposes of civil society? If the administrators of every government are actuated by views of private interest and ambition, how is the welfare and happiness of the community to be the result of such jarring adverse interests?

Therefore, as different orders in government will not produce the good of the whole, we must recur to other principles. I believe it will be found that the form of government, which holds those entrusted with power in the greatest responsibility to their constituents, the best calculated for freemen. A republican, or free government, can only exist where the body of the people are virtuous, and where property is pretty equally divided. In such a government the people are the sovereign and their sense or opinion is the criterion of every public measure; for when this ceases to be the case, the nature of the government is changed, and an aristocracy, monarchy or despotism will rise on its ruin.[5] The highest responsibility is to be attained in a simple structure of government, for the great body of the people never steadily attend to the operations of government, and for want of due information are liable to be imposed on. If you complicate the plan by vari-

9

ous orders, the people will be perplexed and divided in their senti-ment about the source of abuses or misconduct; some will impute it to the senate, others to the house of representatives, and so on, that the interposition of the people may be rendered imperfect or perhaps wholly abortive. But if, imitating the constitution of Pennsylvania, you vest all the legislative power in one body of men (separating the executive and judicial) elected for a short period, and necessarily excluded by rotation from permanency, and guarded from precipi-tancy and surprise by delays imposed on its proceedings, you will create the most perfect responsibility; for then, whenever the people feel a grievance, they cannot mistake the authors, and will apply the remedy with certainty and effect, discarding them at the next elec-tion. This tie of responsibility will obviate all the dangers apprehended from a single legislature, and will the best secure the rights of the people.

Having premised this much, I shall now proceed to the examina-tion of the proposed plan of government, and I trust, shall make it appear to the meanest capacity, that it has none of the essential requi-sites of a free government; that it is neither founded on those balanc-ing restraining powers, recommended by Mr. Adams and attempted in the British constitution, or possessed of that responsibility to its constituents, which, in my opinion, is the only effectual security for the liberties and happiness of the people; but on the contrary, that it is a most daring attempt to establish a despotic aristocracy among free-men, that the world has ever witnessed.

I shall previously consider the extent of the powers intended to be vested in Congress, before I examine the construction of the general government.

It will not be controverted that the legislative is the highest del-egated power in government, and that all others are subordinate to it. The celebrated *Montesquieu* establishes it as a maxim, that legisla-tion necessarily follows the power of taxation. By sect. 8, of the first article of the proposed plan of government, "the Congress are to have power to lay and collect taxes, duties, imposts, and excises, to pay the debts and provide for the common defense and *general welfare* of the United States; but all duties, imposts and excises, shall be uni-form throughout the United States." Now what can be more comprehensive than these words? Not content by other sections of this plan, to grant all the great executive powers of a confederation, and a STANDING ARMY IN TIME OF PEACE, that grand engine of oppression, and moreover the absolute control over the commerce of the United States and all external objects of revenue, such as unlimited imposts upon imports, etc., they are to be vested with every species of *internal* taxation; whatever taxes, duties and excises that they may deem requisite for the *general welfare*, may be imposed on the citizens of these states, levied by the officers of Congress, distributed through every district in America; and the collection would be enforced by the standing army, however grievous or improper they may be. The Congress may construe every purpose for which the State legislatures now lay taxes, to be for the *general welfare*, and thereby seize upon every object of revenue.

The judicial power by Article 3d sect. Ist shall extend to all cases, in law and equity, arising under this constitution, the laws of the United States, and treaties made or which shall be made under their authority; to all cases affecting ambassadors, other public ministers and consuls; to all cases of admiralty and maritime jurisdiction, to controversies to which the United States shall be a party, to controversies between two or more States, between a State and citizens of another State, between citizens of different States, between citizens of the same State claiming lands under grants of different States, and between a State, or the citizens thereof, and foreign States, citizens or subjects.

The judicial power to be vested in one Supreme Court, and in such inferior Courts as the Congress may from time to time ordain and establish.

The objects of jurisdiction recited above are so numerous, and the shades of distinction between civil causes are oftentimes so slight, that it is more than probable that the State judicatories would be wholly superseded; for in contests about jurisdiction, the federal court, as the most powerful, would ever prevail. Every person acquainted with the history of the courts in England, knows by what ingenious sophisms they have, at different periods, extended the sphere of their jurisdiction over objects out of the line of their institution, and contrary to their very nature; courts of a criminal jurisdiction obtaining cognizance in civil causes.

To put the omnipotency of Congress over the State government and judicatories out of all doubt, the 6th article ordains that "this constitution and the laws of the United States which shall be made in pursuance thereof, and all treaties made, or which shall be made under the authority of the United States, shall be the *supreme law of the land*, and the judges in every State shall be bound thereby, anything in the constitution or laws of any State to the contrary notwithstanding."

By these sections the all-prevailing power of taxation, and such extensive legislative and judicial powers are vested in the general government, as must in their operation necessarily absorb the State legislatures and judicatories; and that such was in the contemplation of the framers of it, will appear from the provision made for such event, in another part of it (but that, fearful of alarming the people by so great an innovation, they have suffered the forms of the separate governments to remain, as a blind). By Article Ist sect. 4th, "the times, places and manner of holding elections for senators and representatives, shall be prescribed in each State by the legislature thereof; *but the Congress may at any time, by law, make or alter such regulations, except as to the place of choosing senators.*" The plain construction of which is, that when the State legislatures drop out of sight, from the necessary operation of this government, then Congress are to provide for the election and appointment of representatives and senators.

If the foregoing be a just comment, if the United States are to be melted down into one empire, it becomes you to consider whether such a government, however constructed, would be eligible in so extended a territory; and whether it would be practicable, consistent with freedom? It is the opinion of the greatest writers, that a very extensive country cannot be governed on democratical principles, on any other plan than a confederation of a number of small republics, possessing all the powers of internal government, but united in the management of their foreign and general concerns.

It would not be difficult to prove, that anything short of despotism could not bind so great a country under one government; and that whatever plan you might, at the first setting out, establish, it would issue in a despotism.

12

If one general government could be instituted and maintained on principles of freedom, it would not be so competent to attend to the various local concerns and wants, of every particular district, as well as the peculiar governments, who are nearer the scene, and possessed of superior means of information; besides, if the business of the *whole* union is to be managed by one government, there would not be time. Do we not already see, that the inhabitants in a number of larger States, who are remote from the seat of government, are loudly complaining of the inconveniences and disadvantages they are subjected to on this account, and that, to enjoy the comforts of local government, they are separating into smaller divisions?

Having taken a review of the powers, I shall now examine the construction of the proposed general government.

Article Ist, sect. Ist. "All legislative powers herein granted shall be vested in a Congress of the United States, which shall consist of a senate and house of representatives." By another section, the President (the principal executive officer) has a conditional control over their proceedings.

Sect. 2d. "The house of representatives shall be composed of members chosen every second year, by the people of the several States. The number of representatives shall not exceed one for every 30,000 inhabitants."

The senate, the other constituent branch of the legislature, is formed by the legislature of each State appointing two senators, for the term of six years.

The executive power by Article 2d, sect. Ist, is to be vested in a President of the United States of America, elected for four years: Sec. 2 gives him "power, by and with the consent of the senate to make treaties, provided two-thirds of the senators present concur; and he shall nominate, and by and with the advice and consent of the senate, shall appoint ambassadors, other public ministers and consuls, judges of the Supreme Court, and all other officers of the United States, whose appointments are not herein otherwise provided for, and which shall be established by law, etc." And by another section he has the absolute power of granting reprieves and pardons for treason and all other high crimes and misdemeanors, except in case of impeachment.

The foregoing are the outlines of the plan.

Thus we see, the house of representatives are on the part of the people to balance the senate, who I suppose will be composed of the *better sort*, the *well born*, etc. The number of the representatives (being only one for every 30,000 inhabitants) appears to be too few, either to communicate the requisite information of the wants, local circumstances and sentiments of so extensive an empire, or to prevent corruption and undue influence, in the exercise of such great powers; the term for which they are to be chosen, too long to preserve a due dependence and accountability to their constituents; and the mode and places of their election not sufficiently ascertained, for as Congress have the control over both, they may govern the choice, by ordering the *representatives* of a *whole* State, to be *elected* in *one* place, and that too may be the most *inconvenient*.

The senate, the great efficient body in this plan of government, is constituted on the most unequal principles. The smallest State in the Union has equal weight with the great States of Virginia, Massachusetts or Pennsylvania. The senate, besides its legislative functions, has a very considerable share in the executive; none of the principal appointments to office can be made without its advice and consent. The term and mode of its appointment will lead to permanency; the members are chosen for six years, the mode is under the control of Congress, and as there is no exclusion by rotation, they may be continued for life, which, from their extensive means of influence, would follow of course.[6] The President, who would be a mere pageant of State, unless he coincides with the views of the senate, would either become the head of the aristocratic junto in that body, or its minion; besides, their influence being the most predominant, could the best secure his re-election to office. And from his power of granting pardons, he might screen from punishment the most treasonable attempts on the liberties of the people, when instigated by the senate.

From this investigation into the organization of this government, it appears that it is devoid of all responsibility or accountability to the great body of the people, and that so far from being a regular balanced government, it would be in practice a *permanent* ARISTOCRACY.

The framers of it, actuated by the true spirit of such a government, which ever abominates and suppresses all free inquiry and discussion, have made no provision for the *liberty of the press*, that grand *palladium of freedom*, and *scourge of tyrants*; but observed a total silence on that head. It is the opinion of some great writers, that if the liberty of the press, by an institution of religion or otherwise, could be rendered *sacred*, even in *Turkey*, that despotism would fly before it. And it is worthy of remark that there is no declaration of personal rights, premised in most free constitutions; and that trial by *jury* in *civil* cases is taken away; for what other construction can be put on the following, viz: Article 3d, sect. 2d, "In all cases affecting ambassadors, other public ministers and consuls, and those in which a State shall be party, the Supreme Court shall have *original* jurisdiction. In all the other cases above mentioned, the Supreme Court shall have *appellate* jurisdiction, both as to *law and fact!*" It would be a novelty in jurisprudence, as well as evidently improper, to allow an appeal from the verdict of a jury, on the matter of fact; therefore it implies and allows of a dismission of the jury in civil cases, and especially when it is considered, that jury trial in criminal cases is expressly stipulated for, but not in civil cases.

But our situation is represented to be so *critically* dreadful, that, however reprehensible and exceptionable the proposed plan of government may be, there is no alternative between the adoption of it and absolute ruin. My fellow citizens, things are not at that crisis; it is the argument of tyrants; the present distracted state of Europe secures us from injury on that quarter, and as to domestic dissensions, we have not so much to fear from them, as to precipitate us into this form of government, without it is a safe and a proper one. For remember, of all *possible* evils, that of *despotism* is the *worst* and the most to be dreaded.[7]

Besides, it cannot be supposed that the first essay on so difficult a subject, is so well digested as it ought to be; if the proposed plan, after a mature deliberation, should meet the approbation of the respective States, the matter will end; but if it should be found to be fraught with dangers and inconveniences, a future general Convention, being in possession of the objections, will be the better enabled to plan a suitable government.

"WHO'S HERE SO BASE, THAT WOULD A BONDMAN BE?
IF ANY, SPEAK; FOR HIM HAVE I OFFENDED.
WHO'S HERE SO VILE, THAT WILL NOT LOVE HIS COUNTRY?
IF ANY, SPEAK; FOR HIM HAVE I OFFENDED."

CENTINEL.

To the PEOPLE of PENNSYLVANIA. *Friends, Countrymen, and Fellow Citizens.*

As long as the liberty of the press continues unviolated, and the people have the right of expressing and publishing their sentiments upon every public measure, it is next to impossible to enslave a free nation. The state of society must be very corrupt and base indeed, when the people, in possession of such a monitor as the press, can be induced to exchange the heaven-born blessings of liberty for the galling chains of despotism. Men of an aspiring and tyrannical disposition, sensible of this truth, have ever been inimical to the press, and have considered the shackling of it as the first step towards the accomplishment of their hateful domination, and the entire suppression of all liberty of public discussion, as necessary to its support. For even a standing army, that grand engine of oppression, if it were as numerous as the abilities of any nation could maintain, would not be equal to the purposes of despotism over an enlightened people.

The abolition of that grand palladium of freedom, the liberty of the press, in the proposed plan of government, and the conduct of its authors and patrons, is a striking exemplification of these observations. The reason assigned for the omission of a *bill of rights,* securing the *liberty of the press,* and *other invaluable personal rights,* is an insult on the understanding of the people.

The injunction of secrecy imposed on the members of the late Convention during their deliberations, was obviously dictated by the genius of Aristocracy; it was deemed impolitic to unfold the principles of the intended government to the people, as this would have frustrated the object in view.

The projectors of the new plan, supposed that an ex parte discussion of the subject, was more likely to obtain unanimity in the Convention; which would give it such a sanction in the public opinion, as to banish all distrust, and lead the people into an implicit adoption of it without examination.

The greatest minds are forcibly impressed by the immediate circumstances with which they are connected; the particular sphere men move in, the prevailing sentiments of those they converse with, have an insensible and irresistible influence on the wisest and best of mankind; so that when we consider the abilities, talents, ingenuity

17

and consummate address of a number of members of the late Convention, whose principles are despotic, can we be surprised that men of the best intentions have been misled in the difficult science of government? Is it derogating from the character of the *illustrious and highly revered* WASHINGTON, to suppose him fallible on a subject that must be in a great measure novel to him? As a patriotic hero, he stands unequalled in the annals of time.

The new plan was accordingly ushered to the public with such a splendor of names, as inspired the most unlimited confidence; the people were disposed to receive upon trust, without any examination on their part, what would have proved either a *blessing* or a *curse* to them and their posterity. What astonishing infatuation! to stake their happiness on the wisdom and integrity of any set of men! In matters of infinitely smaller concern, the dictates of prudence are not disregarded! The celebrated *Montesquieu*, in his Spirit of Laws, says, that "slavery is ever preceded by sleep." And again, in his account of the rise and fall of the Roman Empire, page 97, "That it may be advanced as a general rule, that in a free State, whenever a perfect calm is visible, the spirit of liberty no longer subsists." And Mr. *Dickinson*, in his Farmer's Letters, No. XI., lays it down as a maxim, that "A perpetual jealousy respecting liberty is absolutely requisite in all free States."[1]

"Happy are the men, and happy the people, who grow wise by the misfortunes of others. Earnestly, my dear countrymen, do I beseech the author of all good gifts, that you may grow wise in this manner, and I beg leave to recommend to you in general, as the best method of obtaining this wisdom, diligently to study the histories of other countries. You will there find all the arts, that can possibly be practised by cunning rulers, or false patriots among yourselves, so fully delineated, that changing names, the account would serve for your own times."

A *few* citizens of Philadelphia (too few, for the honor of human nature) who had the wisdom to think *consideration* ought to precede *approbation*, and the fortitude to avow that they would take time to judge for themselves on so momentous an occasion, were stigmatized as enemies to their country; as monsters, whose existence ought not to be suffered, and the destruction of them and their houses recommended, as meritorious. The authors of the new plan, conscious that it would not stand the test of enlightened patriotism, tyrannically endeavored to preclude all investigation. If their views were laudable, if they were honest, the contrary would have been their conduct, they would have invited the freest discussion. Whatever specious reasons may be assigned for secrecy during the framing of the plan, no good one can exist for leading the people blindfolded into the implicit adoption of it. Such an attempt does not augur the public good—it carries on the face of it an intention to juggle the people out of their liberties.

The virtuous and spirited exertions of a few patriots have at length roused the people from their fatal infatuation to a due sense of the importance of the measure before them. The glare and fascination of names is rapidly abating, and the subject begins to be canvassed on its own merits; and so serious and general has been the impression of the objection urged against the new plan, on the minds of the people, that its advocates, finding mere declamation and scurrility will no longer avail, are reluctantly driven to defend it on the ground of argument. Mr. *Wilson*, one of the deputies of this State in the late Convention, has found it necessary to come forward.[2] From so able a lawyer, and so profound a politician, what might not be expected, if this act of Convention be the heavenly dispensation which some represent it? Its divinity would certainly be illustrated by one of the principal instruments of the Revelation; for this gentleman has that transcendent merit! But if, on the other hand, this able advocate has failed to vindicate it from the objections of its adversaries, must we not consider it as the production of *frail* and *interested* men.

Mr. *Wilson* has recourse to the most flimsy sophistry in his attempt to refute the charge that the new plan of general government will supersede and render powerless the state governments. His quibble upon the term *Corporation*, as sometimes equivalent to communities which possess sovereignty, is unworthy of him. The same comparison in the case of the British parliament assuming to tax the colonies, is made in the Xth of the Farmer's Letters, and was not misunderstood in 1768 by any.[3] He says that the existence of the proposed federal plan depends on the existence of the State governments, as the senators are to be appointed by the several legislatures,

19

who are also to nominate the electors who choose the President of the United States; and that hence all fears of the several states being melted down into one empire, are groundless and imaginary. But who is so dull as not to comprehend, that *semblance* and *forms* of an ancient establishment may remain, after the *reality* is gone. *Augustus*, by the aid of a great army, assumed despotic power, and notwithstanding this, we find even under Tiberius, Caligula and Nero, princes who disgraced human nature by their excesses, the shadows of the ancient constitution held up to amuse the people. The senate sat as formerly; consuls, tribunes of the people, censors and other officers were annually chosen as before, and the forms of republican government continued. Yet all this was in *appearance* only.—Every *senatus consultum* was dictated by him or his ministers, and every Roman found himself constrained to submit in all things to the despot.

Mr. *Wilson* asks, "What control can proceed from the federal government to shackle or destroy that *sacred palladium* of natural freedom, the *liberty of the press*?" What! Cannot Congress, when possessed of the immense authority proposed to be devolved, restrain the printers, and put them under regulation? Recollect that the omnipotence of the federal legislature over the State establishments, is recognized by a special article, viz.,—"that this Constitution, and the laws of the United States which shall be the *supreme law* of the land; and the judges in every State shall be bound thereby, any thing in the *Constitutions* or laws of any State to the contrary notwithstanding." After such a declaration, what security do the *Constitutions* of the several States afford for the *liberty of the press and other invaluable personal rights*, not provided for by the new plan? Does not this sweeping clause subject everything to the control of Congress?

In the plan of Confederation of 1778, now existing, it was thought proper by Article the 2d, to declare that "each State retains its sovereignty, freedom and independence, and every power, jurisdiction and right, which is not by this Confederation expressly delegated to the United States in Congress assembled." *Positive* grant was not *then* thought sufficiently descriptive and restraining upon Congress, and the omission of such a declaration *now*, when such great devolutions of power are proposed, manifests the design of reducing the several States to shadows. But Mr. Wilson tells you, that every right and power not specially granted to Congress is considered as withheld. How does this appear? Is this principle established by the proper authority? Has the Convention made such a stipulation? By no means. Quite the reverse; the *laws* of Congress are to be "the *supreme law* of the land, any thing in the *Constitutions* or laws of any State to the contrary notwithstanding;" and consequently, would be *paramount* to all *State* authorities. The lust of power is so universal, that a speculative unascertained rule of construction would be a *poor* security for the liberties of the people.

Such a body as the intended Congress, unless particularly inhibited and restrained, must grasp at omnipotence, and before long swallow up the legislative, the executive, and the judicial powers of the several States.

In addition to the respectable authorities quoted in my first number, to show that the right of *taxation* includes all the powers of government, I beg leave to adduce the Farmer's Letters, see particularly letter 9th, in which Mr. Dickinson has clearly proved, that if the British Parliament assumed the power of taxing the colonies, *internally*, as well as *externally*, and it should be submitted to, the several colony legislatures would soon become contemptible, and before long fall into disuse. Nothing, says he, would be left for them to do, higher than to frame by-laws for empounding of cattle or the yoking of hogs.

By the proposed plan, there are divers cases of judicial authority to be given to the courts of the United States, besides the two mentioned by Mr. *Wilson*. In maritime causes about property, jury trial has not been usual; but in suits in *equity*, with all due deference to Mr. *Wilson's* professional abilities, (which he calls to his aid) jury trial, as to facts, is in full exercise. Will this jurisperitus say that if the question in equity should be, did *John Doe* make a will, that the chancellor of England would decide upon it? He well knows that in this case, there being no mode of jury trial before the chancellor, the question would be referred to the court of king's bench for discussion according to the common law, and when the judge in equity should receive the *verdict*, the fact so established could never be re-examined or controverted. Maritime causes and those appertaining to a court of equity, are, however, but *two* of the many and extensive subjects of federal cognizance mentioned in the plan. This jurisdiction

21

will embrace all suits arising under the laws of impost, excise and other revenue of the United States. In England if goods be seized, if a ship be prosecuted for non-compliance with, or breach of the laws of the customs, or those for regulating trade, in the courts of exchequer, the claimant is secured by the transcendent privilege of Englishmen, *trial by a jury of his peers*. Why not in the United States of America? This jurisdiction also goes to all cases under the laws of the United States, that is to say, under all statutes and ordinances of Congress. How far this may extend, it is easy to foresee; for upon the decay of the state powers of legislation, in consequence of the loss of the *purse-strings*, it will be found necessary for the federal legislature to make laws upon every subject of legislation. Hence the state courts of justice, like the barony and hundred courts of England, will be eclipsed and gradually fall into disuse.

The jurisdiction of the federal court goes, likewise, to the laws to be created by treaties, made by the President and Senate (a species of legislation) with other nations; "to all cases affecting foreign ministers and consuls; to controversies wherein the United States shall be a party; to controversies between citizens of different states," as when an inhabitant of *New York* has a demand on an inhabitant of *New Jersey*. This last is a very invidious jurisdiction, implying an improper distrust of the impartiality and justice of the tribunals of the states. It will include all legal debates between foreigners in Britain, or elsewhere, and the people of this country. A reason hath been assigned for it, viz: "That large tracts of land, in neighboring states, are claimed under royal tracts or other grants, disputed by the states where the lands lie, so that justice cannot be expected from the state tribunals." Suppose it were proper indeed to provide for such cases, why include all cases, and for all time to come? Demands as to land for 21 years would have satisfied this. A London merchant shall come to America, and sue for his supposed debt, and the citizen of this country shall be deprived of jury trial, and subjected to an appeal (tho' nothing but the *fact* is disputed) to a court 500 or 1000 miles from home; when if this American has a claim upon an inhabitant of England, his adversary is secured of the privilege of jury trial. This jurisdiction goes also to controversies between any state and its citizens, which, though *probably* not intended, may hereafter be set up as a ground to divest the states, severally, of the trial of criminals; inasmuch as every charge of felony or misdemeanor, is a controversy between the state and a citizen of the same: that is to say, the state is plaintiff and the party accused is defendant in the prosecution. In all doubts about jurisprudence, as was observed before, the paramount courts of Congress will decide, and the judges of the state, being *sub graviore lege*, under the paramount law, must acquiesce.

Mr. *Wilson* says that it would have been impracticable to have made a general rule for jury trial in the civil cases assigned to the federal judiciary, because of the want of uniformity in the mode of jury trial, as practiced by the several states. This objection proves too much, and therefore amounts to nothing. If it precludes the mode of common law in civil cases, it certainly does in criminal. Yet in these we are told "the oppression of government is effectually barred by declaring that in all criminal cases *trial by jury* shall be preserved." Astonishing that provision could not be made for a jury in civil controversies of twelve men, whose verdict should be unanimous, *to be taken form the vicinage*; a precaution which is omitted as to trial of crimes, which may be anywhere in the State within which they have been committed. So that an inhabitant of *Kentucky* may be tried for treason at *Richmond*.

The abolition of jury trial in civil cases, is the more considerable, as at length the courts of Congress will supersede the state courts, when such mode of trial will fall into disuse among the people of the United States.

The northern nations of the European continent have all lost this invaluable privilege: *Sweden*, the last of them, by the artifices of the aristocratic senate, which depressed the king and reduced the house of commons to insignificance. But the nation a few years ago preferring the absolute authority of a monarch to the *vexatious* domination of the *well-born* few, an end was suddenly put to their power.

"The policy of this right of juries, (says Judge Blackstone) to decide upon *fact*, is founded on this: That if the power of judging were entirely trusted with the magistrates, or any select body of men, named by the executive authority, their decisions, in spite of their own natural integrity, would have a bias towards those of their own rank and dignity; for it is not to be expected, that the *few* should be attentive to

23

the rights of the *many*. This therefore preserves in the hands of the people, that share which they ought to have in the administration of justice, and prevents the encroachments of the more powerful and wealthy citizens."

The attempt of governor *Colden*, of New York, before the Revolution, to re-examine the facts and re-consider the *damages*, in the case of *Forsey* against *Cunningham*, produced about the year 1764 a flame of patriotic and successful opposition, that will not be easily forgotten.

To manage the various and extensive judicial authority, proposed to be vested in Congress, there will be one or more inferior courts immediately requisite in each State; and laws and regulations must be forthwith provided to direct the judges—here is a wide door for inconvenience to enter. Contracts made under the acts of the States respectively, will come before courts acting under new laws and new modes of proceedings, not thought of when they were entered into. An inhabitant of Pennsylvania residing at Pittsburgh, finds the goods of his debtor, who resides in Virginia, within the reach of his attachment; but no writ can be had to authorize the marshal, sheriff, or other officer of Congress, to seize the property, about to be removed, nearer than 200 miles: suppose that at Carlisle, for instance, such a writ may be had, meanwhile the object escapes. Or if an inferior court whose judges have ample salaries, be established in every county, would not the expense be enormous? Every reader can extend in his imagination, the instances of difficulty which would proceed from this needless interference with the judicial rights of the separate States, and which as much as any other circumstance in the new plan, implies that the dissolution of their forms of government is designed.

Mr. *Wilson* skips very lightly over the danger apprehended from the standing army allowed by the new plan. This grand machine of power and oppression, may be made a fatal instrument to overturn the public liberties, especially as the funds to support the troops may be granted for *two* years, whereas in Britain the grants ever since the revolution in 1688, have been *from year to year.* A standing army with regular provision of pay and contingencies, would afford a strong temptation to some ambitious man to step up into the throne, and to seize absolute power. The keeping on foot a hired military force *in time of peace*, ought not to be gone into unless *two-thirds* of the members of the federal legislature agree to the necessity of the measure, and adjust the numbers employed. Surely Mr. *Wilson* is not serious when he adduces the instance of the troops now stationed on the Ohio, as a proof of the propriety of a standing army. They are a mere occasional armament for the purpose of restraining divers hostile tribes of savages. It is contended that under the present confederation, Congress possess the power of raising armies at pleasure; but the opportunity which the States severally have of withholding the supplies necessary to keep these armies on foot, is a sufficient check on the *present* Congress.

Mr. *Wilson* asserts, that never was charge made with less reason, than that which predicts the institution of a *baneful aristocracy* in the federal Senate. In my first number, I stated that this body would be a very unequal representation of the several States, that the members being appointed for the long term of six years, and there being no exclusion by rotation, they might be continued for life, which would follow of course from their extensive means of influence, and that possessing a considerable share in the *executive* as well as *legislative*, it would become a *permanent aristocracy*, and swallow up the other orders in the government.

That these fears are not imaginary, a knowledge of the history of other nations, where the powers of government have been injudiciously placed, will fully demonstrate. Mr. *Wilson* says, "the senate branches into two characters; the one legislative and the other executive. In its legislative character it can effect no purpose, without the co-operation of the house of representatives, and in its executive character it can accomplish no object without the concurrence of the president. Thus fettered, I do not know any act which the senate can of itself perform, and such dependence necessarily precludes every idea of influence and superiority." This I confess is very specious, but experience demonstrates that checks in government, unless accompanied with *adequate* power and *independently* placed, prove *merely nominal*, and will be inoperative. Is it probable, that the President of the United States, limited as he is in power, and dependent on the will of the senate, in appointments to office, will either have the *firmness* or *inclination* to exercise his prerogative of a conditional control upon the proceedings of that body, however injurious they may be to the public welfare? It will be his interest to coincide with the views of the senate, and thus become the head of the aristocratic junto. The king of England is a constituent part in the legislature, but although an hereditary monarch, in possession of the whole executive power, including the unrestrained appointment to offices, and an immense revenue, enjoys but in *name* the prerogative of a negative upon the parliament. Even the king of England, circumstanced as he is, has not dared to exercise it for near a century past. The check of the house of representatives upon the senate will likewise be rendered nugatory for want of due weight in the democratic branch, and from their constitution *they* may become so *independent* of the *people* as to be indifferent of its interests: nay, as Congress would have the control over the mode and place of their election, by ordering the representatives of a *whole* state to be elected at *one* place, and that too the most *inconvenient*, the ruling powers may govern the *choice*, and thus the house of representatives may be composed of the *creatures* of the senate. Still the *semblance* of checks may remain, but without *operation*.

This mixture of the legislative and executive moreover highly tends to corruption. The chief improvement in government, in modern times, has been the complete separation of the great distinctions of power; placing the *legislative* in different hands from those which hold the *executive*; and again severing the *judicial* part from the ordinary *administrative*. "When the legislative and executive powers (says Montesquieu) are united in the same person, or in the same body of magistrates, there can be no liberty."

Mr. *Wilson* confesses himself not satisfied with the organization of the federal senate, and apologizes for it, by alleging a sort of compromise. It is well known that some members of convention, apprized of the mischiefs of such a compound of authority, proposed to assign the supreme executive powers to the president and a small council, made personally responsible for every appointment to office, or other act, by having their opinions recorded; and that without the concurrence of the majority of the quorum of this council, the president should not be capable of taking any step. Such a check upon the chief magistrate would admirably secure the power of pardoning, now proposed to be exercised by the president alone, from abuse. For as it is placed he may shelter the traitors whom he himself or his coadjutors in the senate have excited to plot against the liberties of the nation.

The delegation of the power of taxation to Congress, as far as duties on imported commodities, has not been objected to. But to extend this to excises, and every species of internal taxation, would necessarily require so many ordinances of Congress, affecting the body of the people, as would perpetually interfere with the State laws and personal concerns of the people. This alone would directly tend to annihilate the particular governments; for the people fatigued with the operation of two masters would be apt to rid themselves of the weaker. But we are cautioned against being alarmed with imaginary evils, for Mr. *Wilson* has predicted that the great revenue of the United States will be raised by impost. Is there any ground for this? Will the impost supply the sums necessary to pay the interest and principal of the foreign loan, to defray the great additional expense of the new constitution; for the policy of the new government will lead it to institute numerous and lucrative civil offices, to extend its influence and provide for the swarms of expectants (the people having in fact no control upon its disbursements), and to afford pay and support for the proposed standing army, that darling and long-wished for object of the *well-born* of America; and which, if we may judge from the principles of the intended government, will be no trifling establishment, for cantonments of troops in every district of America will be necessary to compel the submission of the people to the arbitrary dictates of the ruling powers? I say, will the impost be adequate? By no means. To answer these there must be excises and other indirect duties imposed, and as land taxes will operate too equally to be agreeable to the wealthy aristocracy in the senate who will be possessed of the government, *poll taxes* will be substituted, as provided for in the new plan; for the doctrine then will be *that slaves ought to pay for wearing their heads*.

As the taxes necessary for these purposes will drain your pockets of every penny, what is to become of that virtuous and meritorious class of citizens, the public creditors? However well disposed the people of the United States may be to do them justice, it would not be in their power; and, *after waiting year after year*, without prospect of the payment of the interest or principal of the debt, they will be constrained to sacrifice their certificates in the purchase of waste lands in the far distant wilds of the western territory.

From the foregoing illustration of the powers proposed to be devolved to Congress, it is evident that the general government would necessarily annihilate the particular governments, and that the security of the personal rights of the people by the state constitutions is superseded and destroyed; hence results the necessity of such security being provided for by a bill of rights to be inserted in the new plan of federal government. What excuse can we then make for the omission of this grand palladium, this barrier between *liberty* and oppression? For universal experience demonstrates the necessity of the most express declarations and restrictions, to protect the rights and liberties of mankind from the silent, powerful and ever-active conspiracy of those who govern.

The new plan, it is true, does propose to secure the people of the benefit of personal liberty by the *habeas corpus*, and trial by jury for all crimes, except in case of impeachment: but there is no declaration, that all men have a natural and unalienable right to worship Almighty God, according to the dictates of their own consciences and understanding; and that no man ought, or of right can be compelled to attend any religious worship, or erect or support any place of worship, or maintain any ministry, contrary to, or against his own free will and consent; and that no authority can or ought to be vested in, or assumed by any power whatever, that shall in any case interfere with, or in any manner control, the right of conscience in the free exercise of religious worship: that the trial by jury in civil causes as well as criminal, and the modes prescribed by the common law for safety of life in criminal prosecutions, shall be held sacred; that the requiring of excessive bail, imposing of excessive fines and cruel and unusual punishments be forbidden; that monopolies in trade or arts, other than to authors of books or inventors of useful arts for a reasonable time, ought not to be suffered; that the right of the people to assemble peaceably for the purpose of consulting about public matters, and petitioning or remonstrating to the federal legislature, ought not to be prevented; that *the liberty of the press be held sacred*; that the people have a right to hold themselves, their houses, papers and possessions free from search or seizure; and that therefore warrants without oaths or affirmations first made affording a sufficient foundation for them, and whereby any officer or messenger may be commanded or required to search suspected places, or to seize any person or his property, not particularly described, are contrary to that right and ought not to be granted; and that standing armies in time of peace are dangerous to liberty; and ought not to be permitted but when absolutely necessary; all which is omitted to be done in the proposed government.

But Mr. *Wilson* says, the new plan does not arrogate perfection, for it provides a mode of alteration and correction, if found necessary. This is one among the numerous deceptions attempted on this occasion. True, there is a mode prescribed for this purpose. But it is barely possible that amendments may be made. The fascination of power must first cease, the nature of mankind undergo a revolution, that is not to be expected on this side of eternity. For to effect this (Art. 6) it is provided, that if *two-thirds* of both houses of the federal legislature shall propose them, or when two thirds of the several States by their legislatures shall apply for them, the federal assembly shall call a convention for proposing amendments, which when ratified by three-fourths of the State legislatures, or conventions, as Congress shall see best, shall control and alter the proposed confederation. Does history abound with examples of a voluntary relinquishment of power, however injurious to the community? No; it would require a general and successful rising of the people to effect anything of this nature. The provision therefore is mere sound.

The opposition to the new plan (says Mr. Wilson) proceeds from interested men, *viz.*, the officers of the state governments. He had before denied that the proposed transfer of powers to Congress would annihilate the state governments. But he here lays aside the masque, and avows the fact. For, the truth of the charge against *them* must entirely rest on such consequence of the new plan. For if the state establishments are to remain unimpaired, why should officers peculiarly connected with them, be interested to oppose the adoption of the new plan? Except the collector of the impost, judge of the admiralty, and the collectors of excise, (none of whom have been reckoned of the opposition) they would otherwise have nothing to apprehend. But the charge is unworthy and may with more propriety be retorted on the expectants of office and emolument under the intended government.

The opposition is not so partial and interested as Mr. *Wilson* asserts. It consists of a respectable yeomanry throughout the union, of characters far removed above the reach of his unsupported assertions. It comprises many worthy members of the late convention, and a majority of the present Congress, for a motion made in that honorable body, for their *approbation* and *recommendation* of the new plan, was after two days' animated discussion, prudently withdrawn by its advocates, and a simple *transmission*[4] of the plan to the several states could only be obtained; yet this has been palmed upon the people as the approbation of Congress; and to strengthen the deception, the bells of the city of Philadelphia were rung for a whole day.

Are Mr. W——n,[5] and many of his coadjutors in the late C——n[6], the disinterested patriots they would have us believe? Is their conduct any recommendation of this plan of government? View them the foremost and loudest on the floor of Congress, in our assembly, at town meetings in sounding its eulogiums:—view them preventing investigation and discussion, and in the most despotic manner endeavoring to compel its adoption by the people, with such precipitancy as to preclude the possibility of a due consideration, and then say whether the motives of these men can be pure.

My fellow citizens, such false detestable *patriots* in every nation, have led their blind confiding country, shouting their applauses, into the jaws of *despotism* and *ruin*. May the wisdom and virtue of the people of America save them from the usual fate of nations.

CENTINEL.

To the PEOPLE OF PENNSYLVANIA.

John 3d, verse 20th.—*"For every one that doeth evil, hateth the light, neither cometh to the light, lest his deeds should be reproved." But "there is nothing covered that shall not be revealed; neither hid that shall not be known. Therefore whatever ye have spoken in darkness, shall be heard in the light: and that which ye have spoken in the ear in closets, shall be proclaimed on the housetops."*—St. Luke, chap. xii, 2d and 3d verses.

Friends, Countrymen, and Fellow Citizens!

The formation of a good government is the greatest effort of human wisdom, actuated by disinterested patriotism; but such is the cursed nature of ambition, so prevalent among men, that it would sacrifice everything to its selfish gratification; hence the fairest opportunities of advancing the happiness of humanity, are so far from being properly improved, that they are too often converted by the votaries of power and domination, into the means of obtaining their nefarious ends. It will be the misfortune of America of adding to the number of examples of this kind, if the proposed plan of government should be adopted; but I trust, short as the time allowed yet for consideration is, you will be so fully convinced of the truth of this, as to escape the impending danger; it is not necessary to strip the monster of its assumed garb, and to exhibit it in its native colours, to excite the universal abhorrence and rejection of every virtuous and patriotic mind.

For the sake of my dear country, for the honor of human nature, I hope and am persuaded that the good sense of the people will enable them to rise superior to the most formidable conspiracy against the liberties of a free and enlightened nation, that the world has ever witnessed. How glorious would be the triumph! How it would immortalize the present generation in the annals of freedom!

The establishment of a government, is a subject of such momentous and lasting concern, that it should not be gone into without the clearest conviction of its propriety, which can only be the result of the fullest discussion, the most thorough investigation and dispassionate consideration of its nature, principles and construction. You are now called upon to make this decision, which involves in it not only your fate, but that of your posterity for ages to come. Your de-

31

termination will either ensure the possession of those blessings which render life desirable, or entail those evils which make existence a curse: that such are the consequences of a wise or improper organization of government, the history of mankind abundantly testifies. If you viewed the magnitude of the object in its true light, you would join with me in sentiment, that the new government ought not to be implicitly admitted. Consider then duly before you leap, for after the Rubicon is once passed, there will be no retreat.

If you were even well assured that the utmost purity of intention predominated in the production of the proposed government, such is the imperfection of human reason and knowledge, that it would not be wise in you to adopt it with precipitation in toto, for all former experience must teach you the propriety of a revision on such occasions, to correct the errors, and supply the deficiencies that may appear necessary. In every government whose object is the public welfare, the laws are subjected to repeated revisions, in some by different orders in the governments, in others by an appeal to the judgement of the people and deliberative forms of procedure. A knowledge of this, as well as of other states, will show that in every instance where a law has been passed without the usual precautions, it has been productive of great inconvenience and evils, and frequently has not answered the end in view, a supplement becoming necessary to supply its deficiencies.

What then are we to think of the motives and designs of those men who are urging the implicit and immediate adoption of the proposed government; are they fearful, that if you exercise your good sense and discernment, you will discover the masqued aristocracy, that they are attempting to smuggle upon you under the suspicious garb of republicanism? When we find that the principal agents in this business are the very men who fabricated the form of government, it certainly ought to be conclusive evidence of their invidious design to deprive us of our liberties. The circumstances attending this matter, are such as should in a peculiar manner excite your suspicion; it might not be useless to take a review of some of them.

In many of the states, particularly in this and the northern states, there are aristocratic juntos of the *well-born few*, who had been zealously endeavoring since the establishment of their constitutions, to humble that offensive *upstart, equal liberty*; but all their efforts were unavailing, the *ill-bred churl* obstinately kept his assumed station.

However, that which could not be accomplished in the several states, is now attempting through the medium of the future Congress. Experience having shown great defects in the present confederation, particularly in the regulation of commerce and maritime affairs; it became the universal wish of America to grant further powers, so as to make the federal government adequate to the ends of its institution. The anxiety on this head was greatly increased, from the impoverishment and distress occasioned by the excessive importations of foreign merchandise and luxuries and consequent drain of specie, since the peace: thus the people were in the disposition of a drowning man; eager to catch at anything that promised relief, however delusory. Such an opportunity for the acquisition of *undue* power has never been viewed with indifference by the ambitious and designing in any age or nation, and it has accordingly been too successfully improved by such men among us. The deputies from this state (with the exception of two) and most of those from the other states in the union, were unfortunately of this complexion, and many of them of such superior endowments, that in an *ex parte* discussion of the subject by specious glosses, they have gained the concurrence of some well disposed men, in whom their country has great confidence, which has given a great sanction to their scheme of power.[1]

A comparison of the authority under which the convention acted, and their form of government, will show that they have despised their delegated power, and assumed sovereignty; that they have entirely annihilated the old confederation, and the particular governments of the several States, and instead thereof have established one general government that is to pervade the union; constituted on the most *unequal* principles, destitute of accountability to its constituents, and as despotic in its nature, as the Venetian aristocracy; a government that will give full scope to the magnificent designs of the *well-born*, a government where tyranny may glut its vengeance on the *low-born*, unchecked by *an odious bill of rights*, as has been fully illustrated in my two preceding numbers; and yet as a blind upon the understandings of the people, they have continued the forms of the particular governments, and termed the whole a confederation of the United

States, pursuant to the sentiments of that profound, but corrupt politician Machiavel, who advises any one who would change the constitution of a State to keep as much as possible to the forms; for then the people seeing the same officers, the same formalities, courts of justice and other outward appearances, are insensible of the alteration, and believe themselves in possession of their old government. Thus Cæsar, when he seized the Roman liberties, caused himself to be chosen dictator (which was an ancient office) continued the senate, the consuls, the tribunes, the censors, and all other offices and forms of the commonwealth; and yet changed Rome from the most free, to the most tyrannical government in the world.

The convention, after vesting all the great and efficient powers of sovereignty in the general government, insidiously declare by section 4th of article 4th, "that the United States shall guarantee to every state in this union, a republican *form* of government;" but of what avail will be the *form*, without the *reality* of freedom?

The late convention, in the majesty of its assumed omnipotence, have not even condescended to submit the plan of the new government to the confederation of the people, the true source of authority; but have called upon them by their several constitutions, to 'assent to and ratify'[2] in toto, what they have been pleased to decree; just as the grand monarque of France requires the parliament of Paris to register his edicts without revision or alteration, which is necessary previous to their execution.

The authors and advocates of the new plan, conscious that its establishment can only be obtained from the ignorance of the people of its true nature, and their unbounded confidence in some of the men concurring, have hurried on its adoption with a precipitation that betrays their design; before many had seen the new plan, and before any had time to examine it, they by their ready minions, attended by some well-disposed but mistaken persons, obtained the subscriptions of the people to papers expressing their entire approbation of, and their wish to have it established; thus precluding them from any consideration; but lest the people should discover the juggle, the elections of the State conventions are urged on at very early days: the proposition of electing the convention for this State in nine days after the date of the resolution for all counties east of Bedford, and supported by three or four of the deputies of the convention, and who were also members of the then assembly, is one of the most extravagant instances of this kind; and even this was only prevented by the secession of nineteen virtuous and enlightened members.[3]

In order to put the matter beyond all recall, they have proceeded a step further; they have made the deputies nominated for the state convention for this city and elsewhere, pledge their sacred honor, previous to their election, that they would implicitly adopt the proposed government in toto. Thus, short as the period is before the final fiat is to be given, consideration is rendered nugatory, and conviction of its dangers or impropriety unavailable. A good cause does not stand in need of such means; it scorns all indirect advantages and borrowed helps, and trusts alone to its own native merit and intrinsic strength: the lion is never known to make use of cunning, nor can a good cause suffer by a free and thorough examination—it is knavery that seeks disguise. Actors do not care that any one should look into the tiring room, nor jugglers or sharpers into their hands or boxes.

Every exertion has been made to suppress discussion by shackling the press; but as this could not be effected in *this* state, the people were warned not to listen to the adversaries of the proposed plan, lest they should impose upon them, and thereby prevent the adoption of this blessed government. What figure would a lawyer make in a court of justice, if he should desire the judges not to hear the counsel of the other side, lest they should perplex the cause and mislead the court? Would not every bystander take it for granted, that he was conscious of the weakness of his client's cause, and that it could not otherwise be defended than by not being understood?

All who are friends to liberty are friends to reason, the champions of liberty; and none are foes to liberty but those who have truth and reason for their foes. He who has dark purposes to serve, must use dark means: light would discover him, and reason expose him: he must endeavor to shut out both, and make them look frightful by giving them ill names.

Liberty only flourishes where reason and knowledge are encouraged: and whenever the latter are stifled, the former is extinguished. In Turkey printing is forbid, enquiry is dangerous, and free speaking is capital; because they are all inconsistent with the nature of the government. Hence it is that the Turks are all stupidly ignorant and are all slaves.

I shall now proceed in the consideration of the construction of the proposed plan of government. By section 4th of article 1st of the proposed government it is declared, "that the times, places, and manner of holding elections for senators and representatives shall be prescribed in each State by the legislature thereof; *but the Congress may at any time by law make or alter such regulations except as to the place of choosing senators.*" Will not this section put it in the power of the future Congress to abolish the suffrage by ballot, so indispensisble in a free governmentf? Montesquieu in his Spirit of Laws, vol. I, page 12 says "that in a democracy there can be no exercise of sovereignty, but by the suffrages of the people, which are their will; now the sovereign's will is the sovereign himself. The laws therefore which establish the right of suffrage, are fundamental to this government. In fact it is as important to regulate in a republic, in what manner, by whom, and concerning what, suffrages are to be given, as it is in a monarchy to know who is the Prince and after what manner he ought to govern." This valuable privilege of voting by ballot ought not to rest on the discretion of the government, but be irrevocably established in the constitution.

Will not the above quoted section also authorize the future Congress to lengthen the terms for which the senators and representatives are to be elected, from 6 and 2 years respectively, to any period, even for life?—as the parliament of England voted themselves from triennial to septinnial; and as the long parliament under Charles the 1st became perpetual?

Section 8th of article 1st, vests Congress with power "to provide for calling forth the militia to execute the laws of the union, suppress insurrections and repel invasions; to provide for organizing, arming, and disciplining the militia, and for governing such part of them as may be employed in the service of the United States, reserving to the States respectively, the appointment of the officers, and the authority of training the militia according to the discipline prescribed by Congress." This section will subject the citizens of these States to the most arbitrary military discipline: even death may be inflicted on the disobedient; in the character of militia, you may be dragged from

36

your families and homes to any part of the continent and for any length of time, at the discretion of the future Congress; and as militia you may be made the unwilling instruments of oppression, under the direction of government; there is no exemption upon account of conscientious scruples of bearing arms, no equivalent to be received in lieu of personal services. The militia of Pennsylvania may be marched to Georgia or New Hampshire, however incompatible with their interests or consciences; in short, they may be made as mere machines as Prussian soldiers.

Section the 9th begins thus:—"The migration or importation of such persons as any of the states, now existing, shall think proper to admit, shall not be prohibited by Congress, prior to the year 1808, but a duty or tax may be imposed on such importation, not exceeding ten dollars for each person." And by the fifth article this restraint is not to be removed by any future convention. We are told that the objects of this article are slaves, and that it is inserted to secure to the southern states the right of introducing negroes for twenty-one years to come, against the declared sense of the other states to put an end to an odious traffic in the human species, which is especially scandalous and inconsistent in a people, who have asserted their own liberty by the sword, and which dangerously enfeebles the districts wherein the laborers are bondsmen. The words, dark and ambiguous, such as no plain man of common sense would have used, are evidently chosen to conceal from Europe, that in this enlightened country, the practice of slavery has its advocates among men in the highest stations. When it is recollected that no poll tax can be imposed on *five* negroes, above what *three* whites shall be charge; when it is considered, that the imposts on the consumption of Carolina field negroes must be trifling, and the excise nothing, it is plain that the proportion of contributions, which can be expected from the southern states under the new constitution, will be unequal, and yet they are to be allowed to enfeeble themselves by the further importation of negroes till the year 1808. Has not the concurrence of the five southern states (in the convention) to the new system, been purchased too dearly by the rest, who have undertaken to make good their deficiencies of revenue, occasioned by their wilful incapacity, without an equivalent?

The general acquiescence of one description of citizens in the proposed government, surprises me much; if so many of the Quakers have become indifferent to the sacred rights of conscience, so amply secured by the constitution of this commonwealth; if they are satisfied to rest this inestimable privilege on the discretion of the future government; yet in a political light they are not acting wisely: in the state of Pennsylvania, they form so considerable a portion of the community, as must ensure them great weight in the government; but in the scale of general empire, they will be lost in the balance.

I intended in this number to have shown from the nature of things, from the opinions of the greatest writers and from the peculiar circumstances of the United States, the impracticability of establishing and maintaining one government on the principles of freedom in so extensive a territory; to have shown, if practicable, the inadequacy of such government to provide for its many and various concerns; and also to have shown that a confederation of small republics, possessing all the powers of internal government, and united in the management of their general and foreign concerns, is the only system of government by which so extensive a country can be governed consistent with freedom: but a writer under the signature of Brutus,[4] in the New York paper, which has been re-published by Messrs. Dunlap and Claypoole,[5] has done this in so masterly a manner, that it would be superfluous in me to add anything on this subject.

My fellow citizens, as a lover of my country, as the friend to mankind, whilst it is yet safe to write, and whilst it is yet in your power to avoid it, I warn you of the impending danger. To this remote quarter of the world has liberty fled. Other countries now subject to slavery, were once as free as we yet are; therefore for your own sakes, for the sake of your posterity, as well as for that of the oppressed of all nations, cherish this remaining asylum of liberty.

CENTINEL.

Philadelphia, November 5th, 1787.

CENTINEL NO. 4

To the PEOPLE OF PENNSYLVANIA. *Friends, Countrymen and Fellow Citizens,*

That the present confederation is inadequate to the objects of the union, seems to be universally allowed. The only question is, what additional powers are wanting to give due energy to the federal government? We should, however, be careful, in forming our opinion on this subject, not to impute the temporary and extraordinary difficulties that have hitherto impeded the execution of the confederation, to defects in the system itself. Taxation is in every government a very delicate and difficult subject; hence it has been the policy of all wise statesmen, as far as circumstances permitted, to lead the people by small beginnings and almost imperceptible degrees, into the habits of taxation; where the contrary conduct has been pursued, it has ever failed of full success, not unfrequently proving the ruin of the projectors. The imposing of a burdensome tax at once on a people, without the usual gradations, is the severest test that any government can be put to; despotism itself has often proved unequal to the attempt. Under this conviction, let us take a review of our situation before and since the revolution. From the first settlement of this country until the commencement of the late war, the taxes were so light and trivial as to be scarcely felt by the people; when we engaged in the expensive contest with Great Britain, the Congress, sensible of the difficulty of levying the moneys necessary to its support, by *direct* taxation, had resource to an anticipation of the public resources, by emitting bills of credit, and thus postponed the necessity of taxation for several years; this means was pursued to a most ruinous length; but about the year 80 or 81, it was wholly exhausted, the bills of credit had suffered such a depreciation from the excessive quantities in circulation, that they ceased to be useful as a medium. The country at this period was very much impoverished and exhausted; commerce had been suspended for near six years; the husbandman, for want of a market, limited his crops to his own subsistence; the frequent calls of the militia and long continuance in actual service, the devastations of the enemy, the subsistence of our own armies, the evils of the depreciation of the paper money, which fell chiefly upon the patriotic and virtuous part of the community, had all concurred to produce great distress throughout America. In this situation of affairs, we still had the same powerful enemy to contend with, who had even more numerous and better appointed armies in the field than at any former time. Our allies were applied to in this exigence, but the pecuniary assistance that we could procure from them was soon exhausted; the only resource now remaining was to obtain by direct taxation, the moneys necessary for our defence. The history of mankind does not furnish a similar instance of an attempt to levy such enormous taxes at once, of a people so wholly unprepared and uninured to them—the lamp of sacred liberty must indeed have burned with unsullied lustre, every sordid principle of the mind must have been then extinct, when the people not only submitted to the grievous impositions, but cheerfully exerted themselves to comply with the calls of their country; their abilities, however, were not equal to furnish the necessary sums—indeed the requisition of the year 1782, amounted to the whole income of their farms and other property, including the means of their subsistence; perhaps the strained exertions of *two* years, would not have sufficed to the discharge of this requisition; how then can we impute the difficulties of the people to a due compliance with the requisitions of Congress, to a defect in the confederation? for any government, however energetic, in similar circumstances, would have experienced the same fate. If we review the proceedings of the states, we shall find that they gave every sanction and authority to the requisitions of Congress that their laws could confer, that they attempted to collect the sums called for in the same manner as is proposed to be done in future by the general government, instead of the State legislatures.

It is a maxim that a government ought to be cautious not to govern over much, for when the cord of power is drawn too tight, it generally proves its destruction. The impracticability of complying with the requisitions of Congress has lessened the sense of obligation and duty in the people, and thus weakened the ties of the union; the opinion of power in a free government is much more efficacious than the exercise of it; it requires the maturity of time and repeated practice to give due energy and certainty to the operations of government, especially to such as affect the purses of the people.

The thirteen Swiss Cantons, confederated by more general and weaker ties than these United States are by the present articles of confederation, have not experienced the necessity of strengthening their union by vesting the general diet with further or greater powers; this national body has only the management of their foreign concerns, and in case of a war can only call by requisition on the several Cantons for the necessary supplies, who are sovereign and independent in every internal and local exercise of government—and yet this rope of sand, as our confederation has been termed, which is so similar to that, has held together for ages without any apparent chasm.

I am persuaded that a due consideration will evince, that the present inefficacy of the requisitions of Congress is not owing to a defect in the confederation, but the peculiar circumstances of the times.

The wheels of the general government having been thus clogged, and the arrearages of taxes still accumulating, it may be asked what prospect is there of the government resuming its proper tone, unless more compulsory powers are granted? To this it may be answered, that the produce of imposts on commerce, which all agree to vest in Congress, together with the immense tracts of land at their disposal, will rapidly lessen and eventually discharge the present encumbrances; when this takes place, the mode by requisition will be found perfectly adequate to the extraordinary exigencies of the union. Congress have lately sold land to the amount of eight millions of dollars, which is a considerable portion of the whole debt.

It is to be lamented that the interested and designing have availed themselves so successfully of the present crisis, and under the specious pretence of having discovered a panacea for all the ills of the people, they are about establishing a system of government, that will prove more destructive to them than the wooden horse filled with soldiers did in ancient times to the city of Troy: this horse was introduced by their hostile enemy the Grecians, by a prostitution of the sacred rites of their religion; in like manner, my fellow citizens, are aspiring despots among yourselves prostituting the name of a Washington to cloak their designs upon your liberties.

I would ask how is the proposed government to shower down those treasures upon every class of citizens, as is so industriously inculcated and so fondly believed? Is it by the addition of numerous and expensive establishments? Is it by doubling our judiciaries, instituting federal courts in every county of every state? Is it by a su-

41

perb presidential court? Is it by a large standing army? In short, is it by putting it in the power of the future government to levy money at pleasure, and placing this government so independent of the people as to enable the administration to gratify every corrupt passion of the mind, to riot on your spoils, without check or control?

A transfer to Congress of the power of imposing imposts on commerce and the unlimited regulation of trade, I believe is all that is wanting to render America as prosperous as it is in the power of any form of government to render her; this properly understood would meet the view of all the honest and well-meaning.

What gave birth to the late Continental Convention? Was it not the situation of our commerce, which lay at the mercy of every foreign power, who from motives of interest or enmity could restrict and control it, without risking a retaliation on the part of America, as Congress was impotent on this subject? Such indeed was the case with respect to Britain, whose hostile regulations gave such a stab to our navigation as to threaten its annihilation: it became the interest of even the American merchant to give a preference to foreign bottoms; hence the distress of our seamen, shipwrights, and every mechanic art dependent on navigation.

By these regulations too we were limited in markets for our produce; our vessels were excluded from their West India Islands, many of our staple commodities were denied entrance in Britain; hence the husbandmen were distressed by the demand for their crops being lessened and their prices reduced. This is the source to which may be traced every evil we experience, that can be relieved by a more energetic government. Recollect the language of complaint for years past, compare the recommendations of Congress founded on such complaints, pointing out the remedy, examine the reasons assigned by the different States for appointing delegates to the late Convention, view the powers vested in that body; they all harmonize in one sentiment, that the due regulation of trade and navigation was the anxious wish of every class of citizens, was the great object of calling the Convention.

This object being provided for by the proposed Constitution, the people overlook and are not sensible of the needless sacrifice they are making for it. Of what avail will be a prosperous state of commerce, when the produce of it will be at the absolute disposal of an arbitrary and unchecked government, who may levy at pleasure the most oppressive taxes; who may destroy every principle of freedom; and may even destroy the privilege of complaining.

If you are in doubt about the nature and principles of the proposed government, view the conduct of its authors and patrons: that affords the best explanation, the most striking comment.

The evil genius of darkness presided at its birth, it came forth under the veil of mystery, its true features being carefully concealed, and every deceptive art has been and is practising to have this spurious brat received as the genuine offspring of heaven-born liberty. So fearful are its patrons that you should discern the imposition, that they have hurried on its adoption with the greatest precipitation; they have endeavored also to preclude all investigation, they have endeavored to intimidate all opposition; by such means as these, have they surreptitiously procured a Convention in this State, favorable to their views; and here again investigation and discussion are abridged, the final question is moved before the subject has been under consideration, an appeal to the people is precluded even in the last resort, lest their eyes should be opened; the Convention have denied the minority the privilege of entering the reasons of their dissent on its journals. Thus despotism is already triumphant, and the genius of liberty is on the eve of her exit, is about bidding an eternal adieu to this once happy people.

After so recent a triumph over British despots, after such torrents of blood and treasure have been spent, after involving ourselves in the distress of an arduous war, and incurring such a debt for the express purpose of asserting the rights of humanity; it is truly astonishing that a set of men among ourselves should have the effrontery to attempt the destruction of our liberties. But in this enlightened age to hope to dupe the people by the arts they are practicing is still more extraordinary.

How do the advocates of the proposed government combat the objections urged against it? Not even by an attempt to disprove them, for that would the more fully confirm their truth: but by a species of reasoning that is very congenial to that contempt of the understandings of the people that they so eminently possess, and which policy cannot even prevent frequent ebullitions of. They seem to think that the oratory and fascination of great names and mere sound will suffice to ensure success; that the people may be diverted from a consideration of the merits of the plan by bold assertions and mere declamation. Some of their writers, for instance, paint the distress of every class of citizens with all the glowing language of eloquence, as if this was a demonstration of the excellence, or even the safety of the new plan, which, notwithstanding the reality of this distress, may be a system of tyranny and oppression. Other writers tell you of the great men who composed the late Convention, and give you a pompous display of their virtues instead of a justification of the plan of government; and others again urge the tyrant's plea, they endeavor to make it a case of necessity, now is the critical moment, they represent the adoption of this government as our only alternative, as the last opportunity we shall have of peaceably establishing a government[1]; they assert it to be the best system that can be formed, and that if we reject it, we will have a worse one or none at all; nay, that if we presume to propose alterations, we shall get into a labyrinth of difficulties from which we cannot be extricated, as no two states will agree in amendments; that therefore it would involve us in irreconcilable discord. But they all sedulously avoid the fair field of argument, a rational investigation into the origination of the proposed government. I hope the good sense of the people will detect the fallacy of such conduct, will discover the base juggle, and with becoming resolution resent the imposition.

That the powers of Congress ought to be strengthened, all allow: but is this a conclusive proof of the necessity to adopt the proposed plan? is it a proof that because the late convention, in the first essay upon so arduous and difficult a subject, harmonized in their ideas, that a future convention will not, or that after a full investigation and mature consideration of the objections, they will not plan a better government and one more agreeable to the sentiments of America, or is it any proof that they can never again agree in any plan? The late convention must indeed have been inspired, as some of its advocates have asserted, to admit the truth of these positions, or even to admit the possibility of the proposed government being such a one as America ought to adopt; for this body went upon original ground, foreign from their intentions or powers; they must therefore have been wholly uninformed of the sentiments of their constituents in respect to this form of government, as it was not in their contemplation when the convention was appointed to erect a new government, but to strengthen the old one. Indeed, they seem to have been determined to monopolize the exclusive merit of the discovery, or rather as if darkness was essential to its success they precluded all communication with the people, by closing their doors; thus the well-disposed members, unassisted by public information and opinion, were induced by those arts that are now practicing on the people, to give their sanction to this system of despotism.

Is there any reason to presume that a new convention will not agree upon a better plan of government? Quite the contrary, for perhaps there never was such a coincidence on any occasion as on the present. The opponents to the proposed plan at the same time in every part of the continent, harmonized in the same objections; such an uniformity of opposition is without example, and affords the strongest demonstration of its solidity. Their objections too are not local, are not confined to the interests of any one particular State to the prejudice of the rest, but with a philanthropy and liberality that reflects lustre on humanity, that dignifies the character of America, they embrace the interests and happiness of the whole Union. They do not even condescend to minute blemishes, but show that the main pillars of the fabric are bad, that the essential principles of liberty and safety are not to be found in it, that despotism will be the necessary and inevitable consequence of its establishment.

CENTINEL.

To the PEOPLE OF PENNSYLVANIA. *Friends, Countrymen and Fellow Citizens.*

Mr. Wilson in a speech delivered in our Convention on Saturday the 24th instant, has conceded, nay forcibly proved, that one consolidated government will not answer for so extensive a territory as the United States includes, that slavery would be the necessary fate of the people under such a government. His words are so remarkable that I cannot forbear reciting them: they are as follows, viz., "The extent of country for which the new constitution was required, produced another difficulty in the business of the federal convention. It is the opinion of some celebrated writers, that to a small territory the democratical, to a middling territory (as Montesquieu has termed it) the monarchical, and to an extensive territory the despotic form of government is best adapted. Regarding then, the wide and almost unbounded jurisdiction of the United States, at first view, the hand of despotism seemed necessary to control, connect, and protect it; and hence the chief embarrassment rose. For, we knew that, although our constituents would cheerfully submit to the legislative restraints of a free government, they would spurn at every attempt to shackle them with despotic power." See page 5 of the printed speech. And again in page 7, he says "Is it probable that the dissolution, of the state governments, and the establishment of one consolidated empire, would be eligible in its nature, and satisfactory to the people in its administration? I think not, as I have given reasons to show that so extensive a territory could not be governed, connected, and preserved, but by the supremacy of despotic power. All the exertions of the most potent emperors of Rome were not capable of keeping that empire together, which, in extent, was far inferior to the dominion of America."

This great point having been now confirmed by the concession of Mr. Wilson, though indeed it was self-evident before, and the writers against the proposed plan of government having proved to demonstration, that the powers proposed to be vested in Congress will necessarily annihilate and absorb the State Legislatures and judiciaries, and produce from their wreck one consolidated government, the question is determined. Every man therefore who has the welfare of his country at heart, every man who values his own liberty and happiness, in short, every description of persons, except those aspiring despots who hope to benefit by the misery and vassalage of their countrymen, must now concur in rejecting the proposed system of government, must now unite in branding its authors with the stigma of eternal infamy. The anniversary of this great escape from the fangs of despotism ought to be celebrated as long as liberty shall continue to be dear to the citizens of America.

I will repeat some of my principal arguments, and add some further remarks on the subject of consolidation:

The Legislature is the highest delegated power in government; all others are subordinate to it. The celebrated Montesquieu established it as a maxim, that legislation necessarily follows the power of taxation. By the 8th sect. of article the ıst, of the proposed government, "the Congress are to have power to lay and collect taxes, duties, imposts, and excises, to pay the debts and provide for the common defence and *general welfare* of the United States." Now what can be more comprehensive than these words? Every species of taxation, whether external or internal, is included. Whatever taxes, duties, and excises that the Congress may deem necessary to the *general welfare* may be imposed on the citizens of these states, and levied by their officers. The Congress are to be the absolute judges of the propriety of such taxes; in short, they may construe every purpose for which the state legislatures now lay taxes, to be for the *general welfare*; they may seize upon every source of taxation, and thus make it impracticable for the states to have the smallest revenue, and if a state should presume to impose a tax or excise that would interfere with a federal tax or excise, Congress may soon terminate the contention by repealing the state law, by virtue of the following section: "To make all laws which shall be necessary and proper for carrying into execution the foregoing powers and all other powers vested by this constitution in the government of the United States, or in any department thereof." Indeed, every law of the states may be controlled by this power. The legislative power granted for these sections is so unlimited in its nature, may be so comprehensive and boundless in its exercise, that this alone would be amply sufficient to carry the coup de grace to the state governments, to swallow them up in the grand vortex of general empire. But the legislative has an able auxiliary in the judicial department, for a reference to my second number will show that this may be made greatly instrumental in effecting a consolidation; as the federal judiciary would absorb all others. Lest the foregoing powers should not suffice to consolidate the United States into one empire, the Convention, as if determined to prevent the possibility of a doubt, as if to prevent all clashing by the opposition of state powers, as if to preclude all struggle for state importance, as if to level all obstacles to the supremacy of universal sway, which in so extensive a territory would be an iron-handed despotism, have ordained by article the 6th, "That this constitution, and the laws of the United States, shall be the *supreme law of the land; and the judges in every state shall be bound thereby, anything in the constitution or laws of any state to the contrary notwithstanding.*"

The words "pursuant to the constitution" will be no restriction to the authority of Congress; for the foregoing sections give them unlimited legislation; their unbounded power of taxation does alone include all others, as whoever has the purse-strings will have full dominion. But the convention has superadded another power, by which the Congress may stamp with the sanction of the constitution every possible law; it is contained in the following clause: "To make all laws which shall be necessary and proper for carrying into execution the foregoing powers, and all other powers vested by this constitution in the government of the United States, or in any department or officer thereof." Whatever law Congress may deem necessary and proper for carrying into execution any of the powers vested in them may be enacted; and by virtue of this clause, they may control and abrogate any and every of the laws of the State governments, on the allegation that they interfere with the execution of any of their powers, and yet these laws will "be made in pursuance of the constitution," and of course will "be the supreme law of the land, and the judges in every State shall be bound thereby, anything in the *constitution* or *laws* of any state to the contrary notwithstanding."

There is no reservation made in the whole of this plan in favor of the rights of the separate States. In the present plan of confederation, made in the year 1778, it was thought necessary by article the 2d to declare that "each State retains its sovereignty, freedom and independence, and every power, jurisdiction and right, which is not by this confederation expressly delegated to the United States in Con-

gress assembled." *Positive* grant was not *then* thought sufficiently
descriptive and restrictive upon Congress, and the omission of such a
declaration now, when such great devolutions of power are proposed,
manifests the design of consolidating the States.

What restriction does Mr. Wilson pretend there is in the new constitution to the supremacy of despotic sway over the United States?
What barrier does he assign for the security of the State governments?
Why truly, a mere cobweb of a limit! by interposing the shield of
what will become mere *form*, to check the *reality* of power. He says,
that the existence of the State governments is essential to the organization of Congress, that the former is made the necessary basis of the
latter, for the federal senators and President are to be appointed by
the State legislatures; and that hence all fears of a consolidation are
groundless and imaginary. It must be confessed as reasons and argument would have been foreign to the defence of the proposed plan of
government, Mr. Wilson has displayed much ingenuity on this occasion; he has involved the subject in all the mazes of sophistry, and by
subtil distinctions, he has established principles and positions, that
exist only in his own fertile imagination. It is a solecism in politics
for two co-ordinate sovereignties to exist together; you must separate the sphere of their jurisdiction or after running the race of dominion for some time, one would necessarily triumph over the other,
but in the meantime the subject of it would be harassed with double
impositions to support the contention; however, the strife between
Congress and the States could not be of long continuance, for the
former has a decisive superiority in the outset, and has moreover the
power by the very constitution itself to terminate it when expedient.

As this necessary connection, as it has been termed, between the
State governments and the general government, has been made a point
of great magnitude by the advocates of the new plan, as it is the only
obstacle alleged by them against a consolidation, it ought to be well
considered. It is declared by the proposed plan, that the federal senators and the electors who choose the President of the United States,
shall be appointed by the State legislatures for the long period of six
and four years respectively; how will this connection prevent the State
legislatures being divested of every important, every efficient power?
may not they, will not they, dwindle into mere boards of appointment

as has ever happened in other nations to public bodies, who, in similar circumstances, have been so weak as to part with the essentials of power? Does not history abound with such instances? And this may be the mighty amount of this inseparable connection which is so much dwelt upon as the security of the State governments. Yet even this shadow of a limit against consolidation may be annihilated by the imperial fiat without any violation of even the forms of the constitution. Article 1st, section 4th, has made a provision for this, when the people are sufficiently fatigued with the useless expense of maintaining the *forms* of departed power and security, and when they shall pray to be relieved from the imposition. This section cannot be too often repeated, as it gives such a latitude to the designing, as it revokes every other part of the constitution that may be tolerable, and as it may enable the administration under it, to complete the system of despotism; it is in the following words, viz: "The times, places and manner of holding elections for senators and representatives shall be prescribed in each State by the legislature thereof; *but the Congress may at any time by law make or alter such regulations, except as to the place of choosing senators.*" The only apparent restriction in this clause is as to the *place* of appointing senators, but even this may be rendered of no avail, for as the Congress have the control over the time of appointment of both senators and representatives, they may, under the pretence of an apprehension of invasion, upon the pretence of the turbulence of what they may style a faction, and indeed pretences are never wanting to the designing, they may postpone the time of the election of the senators and the representatives from period to period to perpetuity; thus they may, and if they may, they certainly will, from the lust of dominion, so inherent in the mind of man, relieve the people from the trouble of attending elections by condescending to create themselves. Has not Mr. Wilson avowed it in fact? Has he not said in the convention that it was necessary that Congress should possess this power as the means of its own preservation? Otherwise, says he, an invasion, a civil war, a faction, or a secession of a minority of the assembly, might prevent the representation of a State in Congress.

The advocates of the proposed government must be hard driven when they represent that because the legislatures of this and the other states have exceeded the due bounds of power, notwithstanding every guard provided by their constitutions; that because the lust of arbitrary sway is so powerful as sometimes to get the better of every obstacle; that therefore we should give full scope to it, for that all restriction to it would be useless and nugatory. And further, when they tell you that a good administration will atone for all the defects in the government, which, say they, you must necessarily have, for how can it be otherwise? your rulers are to be taken from among yourselves. My fellow citizens, these aspiring despots must indeed have a great contempt for your understandings when they hope to gull you out of your liberties by such reasoning; for what is the primary object of government, but to check and control the ambitious and designing? how then can moderation and virtue be expected from men who will be in possession of absolute sway, who will have the United States at their disposal? They would be more than men who could resist such temptation! their being taken from among the people would be no security; tyrants are of native growth in all countries, the greatest bashaw in Turkey has been one of the people, as Mr. Wilson tells you the president-general will be. What consolation would this be when you shall be suffering under his oppression?

CENTINEL.

Philadelphia, Nov., 30, 1787.

Centinel No. 6

To the PEOPLE OF PENNSYLVANIA.

"Man is the glory, jest, and riddle of the world."

POPE.

Incredible transition! the people who, seven years ago, deemed every earthly good, every other consideration, as worthless, when placed in competition with liberty, that heaven-born blessing, that zest of all others; the people, who, actuated by this noble ardor of patriotism, rose superior to every weakness of humanity, and shone with such dazzling lustre amidst the greatest difficulties; who, emulous of eclipsing each other in the glorious assertion of the dignity of human nature, courted every danger, and were ever ready, when necessary, to lay down their lives at the altar of liberty: I say the people, who exhibited so lately a spectacle that commanded the admiration, and drew the plaudits of the most distant nations, are now reversing the picture, are now lost to every noble principle, are about to sacrifice that inestimable jewel, liberty, to the genius of despotism. A *golden phantom* held out to them by the crafty and aspiring despots among themselves, is alluring them into the fangs of arbitrary power; and so great is their infatuation, that it seems as if nothing short of the reality of misery necessarily attendant on slavery, will rouse them from their false confidence, or convince them of the direful deception— but then alas! it will be too late, the chains of depotism will be fast riveted and all escape precluded.

For years past, the harpies of power have been industriously inculcating the idea that all our difficulties proceed from the impotency of Congress, and have at length succeeded to give to this sentiment almost universal currency and belief: the devastations, losses and burthens occasioned by the late war; the excessive importations of foreign merchandise and luxuries, which have drained the country of its specie and involved it in debt, are all overlooked, and the inadequacy of the powers of the present confederation is erroneously supposed to be the only cause of our difficulties; hence persons of every description are revelling in the anticipation of the halcyon days consequent on the establishment of the new constitution. What gross deception and fatal delusion! Although very considerable benefit might be derived from strengthening the hands of Congress, so as to

52

enable them to regulate commerce, and counteract the adverse restrictions of other nations, which would meet with the concurrence of all persons; yet this benefit is accompanied in the new constitution with the scourge of despotic power, that will render the citizens of America tenants at will of every species of property, of every enjoyment, and make them the mere drudges of government. The gilded bait conceals corrosives that will eat up their whole substance.

Since the late able discussion, all are now sensible of great defects in the new constitution, are sensible that power is thereby granted without limitations or restriction; yet such is the impatience of the people to reap the golden harvest of regulated commerce, that they will not take time to secure their liberty and happiness, nor even to secure the benefit of the expected wealth; but are weakly trusting their every concern to the discretionary disposal of their future rulers: are content to risk every abuse of power, because they are promised a good administration, because moderation and self-denial are the characteristic features of men in possession of absolute sway. What egregious folly! What superlative ignorance of the nature of power does such conduct discover.

History exhibits this melancholy truth, that slavery has been the lot of nearly the whole of mankind in all ages, and that the very small portion who have enjoyed the blessings of liberty, have soon been reduced to the common level of slavery and misery. The cause of this general vassalage may be traced to a principle of human nature, which is more powerful and operative than all the others combined; it is that lust of dominion that is inherent in every mind, in a greater or less degree; this is so universal and ever active a passion as to influence all our ancestors; the different situation and qualifications of men only modifies and varies the complexion and operation of it.

For this darling pre-eminence and superiority, the merchant, already possessed of a competency, adventures his all in the pursuit of greater wealth; it is for this that men of all descriptions, after having amassed fortunes, still persevere in the toils of labor; in short, this is the great principle of exertion in the votaries of riches, learning, and fame.

In a savage state, pre-eminence is the result of bodily strength and intrepidity, which compels submission from all such as have the misfortune to be less able; therefore the great end of civil government is to protect the weak from the oppression of the powerful, to put every man upon the level of equal liberty; but here again the same lust of dominion by different means frustrates almost always this salutary intention. In a polished state of society, wealth, talents, address and intrigue are the qualities that attain superiority in the great sphere of government.

The most striking illustration of the prevalence of this lust of dominion is, that the most strenuous assertors of liberty in all ages, after successfully triumphing over tyranny, have themselves become tyrants, when the unsuspicious confidence of an admiring people has entrusted them with unchecked power. Rare are the instances of self denial, or consistency of conduct in the votaries of liberty when they have become possessed of the reins of authority; it has been the peculiar felicity of this country, that her *great Deliverer* did not prove a *Cromwell* nor a *Monk*.

Compare the declarations of the most zealous assertors of *religious* liberty, whilst under the lash of persecution, with their conduct when in power; you will find that even the benevolence and humility inculcated in the gospels, prove no restraint upon this love of domination. The mutual contentions of the several sects of religion in England some ages since, are sufficient evidence of this truth.

The annals of mankind demonstrate the precarious tenure of privileges and property dependent upon the will and pleasure of rulers; these illustrate the fatal danger of relying upon the moderation and self-denial of men exposed to the temptations that the Congress under the new constitution will be. The lust of power or dominion is of that nature as seeks to overcome every obstacle, and does not remit its exertions whilst any object of conquest remains; nothing short of the plenitude of dominion will satisfy this cursed demon. Therefore, liberty is only to be preserved by a due responsibility in the government, and by the constant attention of the people; whenever that responsibility has been lessened or this attention remitted, in the same degree has arbitrary sway prevailed.

The celebrated *Montesquieu* has warned mankind of the danger of an implicit reliance on rulers; he says that "a perpetual jealousy respecting liberty, is absolutely requisite in all free states," and again, "that slavery is ever preceded by sleep."

I shall conclude this number with an extract from a speech delivered by Lord *George Digby*, afterwards *Earl* of *Bristol*, in the *English* Parliament, on the triennial bill in the year 1641, viz: "It hath been a maxim among the wisest legislators that whoever means to settle good laws must proceed in them with a sinister opinion of all mankind; and suppose that whoever is not wicked, it is for want only of the opportunity. It is that opportunity of being ill, Mr. Speaker, that we must take away, if ever we mean to be happy, which can never be done but by *the frequency of parliament.*

"No State can wisely be confident of any public minister's continuing good, longer than the rod is held over him.

"Let me appeal to all those that were present in this house at the agitation of the *petition of right.* And let them tell themselves truly of whose promotion to the management of public affairs do they think the generality would, at that time, have had better hopes than of Mr. *Noy* and Sir *Thomas Wentworth*; both having been at that time and in that business, as I have heard, most keen and active patriots, and the latter of them, to the eternal aggravation of his infamous treachery to the commonwealth be it spoken, the first mover and insisted to have this clause added to the *petition of right*, viz:

"That for the comfort and safety of his subjects his Majesty would be pleased to declare his will and pleasure, that all his ministers should serve him according to the laws and statutes of the realm.

"And yet, Mr. Speaker, to whom now can all the inundations upon our *liberties*, under pretence of law, and the late shipwreck at once of all our property, be attributed more than to Noy, and all those other mischiefs whereby this monarchy hath been brought almost to the brink of destruction so much to any as to that *grand apostate* to the commonwealth, the new Lieutenant of Ireland, Sir Thomas Wentworth? Let every man but consider those men as once they were."—British Liberties, pages 184 and 185.

CENTINEL.

Philadelphia, December 22, 1787.

To the PEOPLE OF PENNSYLVANIA. *Friends and Fellow Citizens*:

The admiring world lately beheld the sun of liberty risen to meridian splendor in this western hemisphere, whose cheering rays began to dispel the glooms of even trans-atlantic despotism; the patriotic mind, enraptured with the glowing scene, fondly anticipated an universal and eternal day to the orb of freedom; but the horizon is already darkened and the glooms of slavery threaten to fix their empire. How transitory are the blessings of this life! Scarcely have four years elapsed since these United States, rescued from the domination of foreign despots by the unexampled heroism and perseverance of its citizens at such great expense of blood and treasure, when they are about to fall a prey to the machinations of a profligate junto at home, who seizing the favorable moment when the temporary and extraordinary difficulties of the people have thrown them off their guard and lulled that jealousy of power so essential to the preservation of freedom, have been too successful in the sacrilegious attempt; however I am confident that this formidable conspiracy will end in the confusion and infamy of its authors; that if necessary, the avenging sword of an abused people will humble these aspiring despots to the dust, and that their fate, like that of Charles the First of England, will deter such attempts in future, and prove the confirmation of the liberties of America until time shall be no more.

One would imagine by the insolent conduct of these harpies of power that they had already triumphed over the liberties of the people, that the chains were riveted and tyranny established. They tell us all further opposition will be vain, as this state has passed the Rubicon. Do they imagine the freemen of Pennsylvania will be thus trepanned out of their liberties, that they will submit without a struggle? They must indeed be inebriated with the lust of dominion to indulge such chimerical ideas. Will the act of one-sixth of the people and this too founded on deception and surprise bind the community? Is it thus that the altar of liberty, so recently crimsoned with the blood of our worthies, is to be prostrated and despotism reared on its ruins? Certainly not. The solemn mummery that has been acting in the name of the people of Pennsylvania will be treated with the deserved contempt; it has served indeed to expose the principles of the men concerned, and to draw a line of discrimination between the real and affected patriots.

Impressed with a high opinion of the understanding and spirit of my fellow citizens, I have in no stage of this business entertained a doubt of its eventual defeat; the momentary delusion, arising from an unreserved confidence placed in some of the characters whose names sanctioned this scheme of power, did not discourage me: I foresaw that this blind admiration would soon be succeeded by rational investigation, which, stripping the monster of its gilded covering, would discover its native deformity.

Already the enlightened pen of patriotism, aided by an able public discussion, has dispelled the mist of deception, and the great body of the people are awakened to a due sense of their danger, and are determined to assert their liberty, if necessary by the sword, but this mean need not be recurred to, for who are their enemies? A junto composed of the lordly and high-minded gentry of the profligate and the needy office-hunters; of men principally who in the late war skulked from the common danger. Would such characters dare to face the majesty of a free people? No. All the conflict would be between the offended justice and generosity of the people, whether these sacrilegious invaders of their dearest rights should suffer the merited punishment or escape with an infamous contempt?

However, as additional powers are necessary to Congress, the people will no doubt see the expediency of calling a convention for this purpose as soon as may be by applying to their representatives in assembly at their next session to appoint a suitable day for the election of such Convention.

Philadelphia, December 27, 1787.   CENTINEL.

To the PEOPLE OF PENNSYLVANIA. *Fellow Citizens.*

Under the benign influence of liberty, this country, so recently a rugged wilderness and the abode of savages and wild beasts, has attained to a degree of improvement and greatness, in less than two ages, of which history furnishes no parallel. It is here that human nature may be viewed in all its glory; man assumes the station designed him by the creation, a happy equality and independency pervades the community, it is here the human mind, untrammeled by the restraints of arbitrary power, expands every faculty: as the field to fame and riches is open to all, it stimulates universal exertion, and exhibits a lively picture of emulation, industry and happiness. The unfortunate and oppressed of all nations, fly to this grand asylum, where liberty is ever protected, and industry crowned with success.

But as it is by comparison only that men estimate the value of any good, they are not sensible of the worth of those blessings they enjoy, until they are deprived of them; hence from ignorance of the horrors of slavery, nations, that have been in possession of that rarest of blessings, liberty, have so easily parted with it: when groaning under the yoke of tyranny what perils would they not encounter, what consideration would they not give to regain the inestimable jewel they had lost; but the jealousy of despotism guards every avenue to freedom, and confirms its empire at the expense of the devoted people, whose property is made instrumental to their misery, for the rapacious hand of power seizes upon every thing; despair presently succeeds, and every noble faculty of the mind being depressed, and all motive to industry and exertion being removed, the people are adapted to the nature of the government, and drag out a listless existence.

If ever America should be enslaved it will be from this cause, that they are not sensible of their peculiar felicity, that they are not aware of the value of the heavenly boon, committed to their care and protection, and if the present conspiracy fails, as I have no doubt will be the case, it will be the triumph of reason and philosophy, as these United States have never felt the iron hand of power, nor experienced the wretchedness of slavery.

The conspirators against our liberties have presumed too much on the maxim that nations do not take the alarm, until they feel oppression; the enlightened citizens of America have on two memorable occasions convinced the tyrants of Europe that they are endued with the faculty of foresight, that they will jealously guard against the first introduction of tyranny, however speciously glossed over, or whatever appearance it may assume. It was not the mere amount of *the duty on stamps*, or *tea* that America opposed, they were considered as signals of approaching despotism, as precedents whereon the superstructure of arbitrary sway was to be reared.

Notwithstanding such illustrious evidence of the good sense and spirit of the people of these United States, and contrary to all former experience of mankind, which demonstrates that it is only by gradual and imperceptible degrees that nations have hitherto been enslaved, except in case of conquest by the sword, the authors of the present conspiracy are attempting to seize upon absolute power at one grasp; impatient of dominion they have adopted a decisive line of conduct, which, if successful, would obliterate every trace of liberty. I congratulate my fellow citizens that the infatuated confidence of their enemies has so blinded their ambition that their defeat must be certain and easy, if imitating the refined policy of successful despots, they had attacked the citadel of liberty by sap, and gradually undermined its outworks, they would have stood a fairer chance of effecting their design; but in this enlightened age thus rashly to attempt to carry the fortress by storm, is folly indeed. They have even exposed some of their batteries prematurely, and thereby unfolded every latent view, for the unlimited power of taxation would alone have been amply sufficient for every purpose; by a proper application of this, the will and pleasure of the rulers would of course have become the supreme law of the land; therefore there was no use in portraying the ultimate object by superadding the form to reality of supremacy in the following clause, viz: That which empowers the new Congress to make all laws that may be necessary and proper for carrying into execution any of their powers, by virtue of which every possible law will be constitutional, as they are to be the sole judges of the propriety of such laws, that which ordains that their acts shall be the supreme law of the land, anything in the laws or constitution of any State to the contrary notwithstanding; that which gives Congress the absolute control over time and mode of its appointment and election, whereby, independent of any other means, they may establish hereditary despotism; that which authorizes them to keep on foot at all times a standing army; and that which subjects the militia to absolute command, and to accelerate the subjugation of the people, trial by jury in civil cases and the liberty of the press are abolished.

So flagrant, so audacious a conspiracy against the liberties of a free people is without precedent. Mankind in the darkest ages have never been so insulted; even then, tyrants found it necessary to pay some respect to the habits and feelings of the people, and nothing but the name of a Washington could have occasioned a moment's hesitation about the nature of the new plan, or saved its authors from the execration and vengeance of the people, which eventually will prove an aggravation of their treason; for America will resent the imposition practiced upon the unsuspicious zeal of her *illustrious deliverer*, and vindicate her character from the aspersions of these enemies of her happiness and fame.

The advocates of this plan have artfully attempted to veil over the true nature and principles of it with the names of those respectable characters that by consummate cunning and address they have prevailed upon to sign it, and what ought to convince the people of the deception and excite their apprehensions, is that with every advantage which education, the science of government and of law, the knowledge of history and superior talents and endowments, furnish the authors and advocates of this plan with, they have from its publication exerted all their power and influence to prevent all discussion of the subject, and when this could not be prevented they have constantly avoided the ground of argument and recurred to declamation, sophistry and personal abuse, but principally relied upon the magic of names. Would this have been their conduct, if their cause had been a good one? No, they would have invited investigation and convinced the understandings of the people.

But such policy indicates great ignorance of the good sense and spirit of the people, for if the sanction of every convention throughout the union was obtained by the means these men are practising; yet their triumph would be momentary, the favorite object would still elude their grasp; for a good government founded on fraud and deception could not be maintained without an army sufficiently powerful to compel submission, which the *well-born* of America could not speedily accomplish. However the complexion of several of the more considerable States does not promise even this point of success. The Carolinas, Virginia, Maryland, New York and New Hampshire have by their wisdom in taking a longer time to deliberate, in all probability saved themselves from the disgrace of becoming the dupes of this gilded bait, as experience will evince that it need only be properly examined to be execrated and repulsed.

The merchant, immersed in schemes of wealth, seldom extends his views beyond the immediate object of gain; he blindly pursues his seeming interest, and sees not the latent mischief; therefore it is, that he is the last to take the alarm when public liberty is threatened. This may account for the infatuation of some of our merchants, who, elated with the imaginary prospect of an improved commerce under the new government, overlook all danger: they do not consider that commerce is the hand-maid of liberty, a plant of free growth that withers under the hand of despotism, that every concern of individuals will be sacrificed to the gratification of the men in power, who will institute injurious monopolies and shackle commerce with every device of avarice; and that property of every species will be held at the will and pleasure of rulers.

If the nature of the case did not give birth to these well founded apprehensions, the principles and characters of the authors and advocates of the measure ought. View the monopolizing spirit of the principal of them. See him converting a bank, instituted for common benefit, to his own and creatures' emoluments, and by the aid thereof, controlling the credit of the state, and dictating the measures of government. View the vassalage of our merchants, the thraldom of the city of Philadelphia, and the extinction of that spirit of independency in most of its citizens so essential to freedom. View this Collosus attempting to grasp the commerce of America and meeting with a sudden repulse—in the midst of his immense career, receiving a shock that threatens his very existence. View the desperate fortunes of many of his coadjutors and defendants, particularly the bankrupt situation of the principal instrument under the *great man* in promoting the new government, whose superlative arrogance, ambition and rapacity, would need the spoils of thousands to gratify; view his towering aspect—he would have no bowels of compassion for the oppressed, he would *overlook* all their sufferings. Recollect the strenuous and un-remitted exertions of these men, for years past, to destroy our admirable Constitution, whose object is to secure equal liberty and advantages to all, and the great obstacle in the way of their ambitious schemes, and then answer whether these apprehensions are chimerical, whether such characters will be less avaricious, more moderate, when the privileges, property, and every concern of the people of the United States shall lie at their mercy, when they shall be in possession of absolute sway?

Philadelphia, December 29, 1787.   CENTINEL.

To the PEOPLE OF PENNSYLVANIA. *Fellow Citizens,*

You have the peculiar felicity of living under the most perfect system of local government in the world; prize then this invaluable blessing as it deserves. Suffer it not to be wrested from you, and the scourge of despotic power substituted in its place, under the specious pretence of vesting the general government of the United States with necessary power; that this would be the inevitable consequence of the establishment of the new constitution, the least consideration of its nature and tendency is sufficient to convince every unprejudiced mind. If you were sufficiently impressed with your present favored situation, I should have no doubt of a proper decision of the question in discussion.

The highest illustration of the excellence of the constitution of this commonwealth, is, that from its first establishment, the ambitious and profligate have been united in a constant conspiracy to destroy it; so sensible are they that it is their great enemy, that it is the great palladium of equal liberty, and the property of the people from the rapacious hand of power. The annals of mankind do not furnish a more glorious instance of the triumph of patriotism over the lust of ambition aided by most of the wealth of the State. The few generally prevail over the many by uniformity of council, unremitted and persevering exertion, and superior information and address; but in Pennsylvania the reverse has happened; here the *well-born* have been baffled in all their efforts to prostrate the altar of liberty for the purpose of substituting their own insolent sway that would degrade the freemen of this State into servile dependence upon the *lordly* and *great*. However it is not the nature of ambition to be discouraged; it is ever ready to improve the first opportunity to rear its baneful head and with irritated fury to wreak its vengeance on the votaries of liberty. The present conspiracy is a continental exertion of the *well-born* of America to obtain that darling domination, which they have not been able to accomplish in their respective States. Of what complexion were the deputies of this State in the general convention? *Six* out of *eight* were the inveterate enemies of our inestimable constitution, and the principals of that faction that for ten years past have kept the people in continual alarm for their liberties.[1] Who are the advocates of the new constitution in this State? They consist of the same faction, with the addition of a few deluded well-meaning men, but whose number is daily lessening.

These conspirators have come forward at a most favorable conjuncture, when the state of public affairs has lulled all jealousy of power: Emboldened by the sanction of the august name of a *Washington*, that they have prostituted to their purpose, they have presumed to overleap the usual gradations to absolute power, and have attempted to seize at once upon the supremacy of dominion. The new instrument of government does indeed make a fallacious parade of some remaining privileges, and insults the understandings of the people with the semblance of liberty in some of its artful and deceptive clauses, which form but a flimsy veil over the reality of tyranny, so weakly endeavored to be concealed from the eye of freedom. For, of what avail are the few inadequate stipulations in favor of the rights of the people, when they may be effectually counteracted and destroyed by virtue of other clauses, when these enable the rulers to renounce all dependence on their constituents, and render the latter tenants at will of every concern? The new constitution is in fact a *carte blanche*, a surrender at discretion to the will and pleasure of our rulers: as this has been demonstrated to be the case, by the investigation and discussion that have taken place, I trust the same good sense and spirit which have hitherto enabled the people to triumph over the wiles of ambition, will be again exerted for their salvation. The accounts from various parts of the country correspond with my warmest hopes, and justify my early predictions of the eventual defeat of this scheme of power and office making.

The genius of liberty has sounded the alarm, and the dormant spirit of her votaries is reviving with enthusiastic ardor; the like unanimity which formerly distinguished them in their conflict with foreign despots, promises to crown their virtuous opposition on the present occasions, with signal success. The structure of despotism that has been reared in this state, upon deception and surprise, will vanish like the baseless fabric of a dream and leave not a trace behind.[2]

The parasites and tools of power in Northampton County ought to take warning from the fate of the Carlisle junto, lest like them, they experience the resentment of an injured people. I would advise them not to repeat the imposition of a set of fallacious resolutions as the sense of that county, when in fact, it was the act of a despicable few, with Alexander Paterson at their head, whose achievements at Wyoming, as the meaner instrument of unfeeling avarice, have rendered infamously notorious; but yet, like the election of a Mr. Sedgwick for the little town of Stockbridge, which has been adduced as evidence of the unanimity of the western counties of Massachusetts State in favor of the new Constitution, when the fact is far otherwise, this act of a few individuals will be sounded forth over the continent as a testimony of the zealous attachment of the county of Northampton to the new Constitution. By such wretched and momentary deceptions do these harpies of power endeavor to give the complexion of strength to their cause. To prevent the detection of such impositions, to prevent the reflection of the rays of light from State to State, which, producing general illumination, would dissipate the mist of deception, and thereby prove fatal to the new Constitution, all intercourse between the patriots of America is as far as possible cut off; whilst on the other hand, the conspirators have the most exact information, a common concert is everywhere evident; they move in unison. There is so much mystery in the conduct of these men, such systematic deception and fraud characterizes all their measures, such extraordinary solicitude shown by them to precipitate and surprise the people into a blind and implicit adoption of this government, that it ought to excite the most alarming apprehensions in the minds of all those who think their privileges, property, and welfare worth securing.

It is a fact that can be established, that during almost the whole of the time that the late convention of this State was assembled, the newspapers published in New York by Mr. Greenleaf, which contains the essays written there against the new government, such as the patriotic ones of Brutus, Cincinnatus, Cato,[3] etc., sent as usual by the printer of that place to the printers of this city, miscarried in their conveyance, which prevented the republication in this State of many of these pieces; and since that period great irregularity prevails, and I stand informed that the printers in New York complain that the free and independent newspapers of this city do not come to hand; whilst on the contrary we find the devoted vehicles of despotism pass uninterrupted. I would ask what is the meaning of the new arrangement at the post-office which abridges the circulation of newspapers at this momentous crisis, when our every concern is dependent upon a proper decision of the subject in discussion. No trivial excuse will be admitted; the Centinel will, as from the first approach of despotism, warn his countrymen of the insidious and base stratagems that are practicing to hood wink them out of their liberties.

The more I consider the manoeuvres that are practicing, the more am I alarmed—foreseeing that the juggle cannot long be concealed, and that the spirit of the people will not brook the imposition, they have guarded as they suppose against any danger arising from the opposition of the people and rendered their struggles for liberty impotent and ridiculous. What otherwise is the meaning of disarming the militia, for the purpose as it is said of repairing their muskets at such a particular period? Does not the timing of the measure determine the intention? I was ever jealous of the select militia, consisting of infantry and troops of horse, instituted in this city and in some of the counties, without the sanction of law, and officers principally by the devoted instruments of the well born, although the illustrious patriotism of one of them has not corresponded with the intention of appointing him. Are not these corps provided to suppress the first efforts of freedom, and to check the spirit of the people until a regular and sufficiently powerful military force shall be embodied to rivet the chains of slavery on a deluded nation? What confirms these apprehensions is the declaration of a certain major, an active instrument in this business, and the echo of the principal conspirators, who has said he should deem the cutting off of five thousand men, as a small sacrifice, a cheap purchase for the establishment of the new Constitution.

Philadelphia, January 5, 1788. CENTINEL.

To the PEOPLE OF PENNSYLVANIA. *Fellow Citizens.*

What illustrious evidence and striking demonstration does the present momentous discussion afford of the inestimable value of the liberty of the press? No doubt now remains, but that it will prove the rock of our political salvation. Despotism, with its innumerable host of evils, by gliding through the mist of deception, had gained some of the principal works, had made a lodgment in the very citadel of liberty before it was discovered, and was near carrying the fortress by surprise; at this imminent alarming crisis the centries from the watch-towers sounded the alarm, and aroused the dormant votaries of liberty to a due sense of their danger; who, with an alacrity and spirit suited to the exigence, answered to the call, repulsed the enemy, dislodged it from most of its acquisitions, and nothing is now wanting to a total rout and complete defeat, but a general discharge from the artillery of freedom. As the shades of night fly before the approach of the radiant sun, so does despotism before the majesty of enlightened truth; wherever free discussion is allowed, this is invariably the consequence. Since the press has been unshackled in Pennsylvania, what an astonishing transition appears in the sentiments of the people! Infatuation is at an end, execration and indignation have succeeded to blind admiration and mistaken enthusiasm. The rampant insolence of the conspirators is prostrated, black despair has taken possession of many of them, their countenances proclaim their defeat, and express serious apprehension for their personal safety from the rising resentment of injured freemen.

James, the Caledonian[1] lieutenant general of the myrmidons of power, under Robert,[2] the cofferer, who, with his aid-de-camp, *Gouvero*,[3] the cunning man, has taken the field in Virginia. I say James, in this exigence summonses a grand council of his partisans in this city and represents in the most pathetic moving language, the deplorable situation of affairs, stimulates them to make a vigorous effort to recover the ground they have lost and establish their empire; that for this purpose a generous contribution must be made by all those who expect to taste the sweets of power, or share in the fruits of dominion, in order to form a fund adequate to the great design, that may put them in possession of the darling object; then recommends that a committee be appointed of those who are gifted with Machiavellian talents of those who excel in ingenuity, artifice, sophistry and the refinements of falsehood, who can assume the pleasing appearance of truth and bewilder the people in all the mazes of error; and as the talk will be arduous, and requires various abilities and talents, the business ought to be distributed, and different parts assigned to other members of the committee, as they may be respectively qualified; some by ingenious sophisms to explain away and counteract those essays of patriotism that have struck such general convictions; some to manufacture extracts of letters and notes from correspondents, to give the complexion of strength to their cause, by representing the unanimity of all corners of America in favor of the new constitution; and others to write reams of letters to their tools in every direction, furnishing them with the materials of propagating error and deception; in short, that this committee ought to make the press groan and the whole country reverberate with their productions; thus to overpower truth and liberty by the din of empty sound and the delusion of falsehood.

The conspirators, deceived by their first success, grounded on the unreserved confidence of the people, do not consider that with the detection of their views all chance of success is over; that suspicion once awakened is not so soon to be lulled, but with eagle eye will penetrate all their wiles, and detect their every scheme, however deeply laid or speciously glossed. The labors of their committee will be unavailing; the point of deception is passed, the rays of enlightened patriotism have diffused general illumination. However, this new effort will serve to show the perseverance of ambition and the necessity of constant vigilance in the people for the preservation of their liberty.

Already we recognize the ingenuity and industry of this committee; the papers teem with paragraphs, correspondents, etc., that exhibit a picture which bears no resemblance to the original. If we view this mirror for the representation of the sentiments of the people, a perfect harmony seems to prevail: every body in every place is charmed with the new Constitution—considers it as a gift from heaven, as their only salvation, etc., etc., etc., and I am informed expresses are employing to waft the delusion to the remotest corners. Such a scene of bustle, lying, and activity, was never exhibited since the days of Adam. The contributions to the grand fund are so great, that it is whispered a magazine of all the apparatus of war is to be immediately provided, and if all other means fail, force is to be recurred to, which they hope will successfully terminate the disagreeable discussion of the rights of mankind, of equal liberty, etc., and thus establish a due subordination to the *well born few*.

CENTINEL.

To the PEOPLE OF PENNSYLVANIA. *Fellow Citizens.*

The arguments upon which the advocates of the new constitution the most dwell, are the distresses of the community, the evils of anarchy, and the horrible consequences that would ensue from the dissolution of the union of the States, and the institution of separate confederacies or republics: The unanimity of the federal convention, and the sanction of great names, can be no further urged as an argument after the exposition made by the attorney-general of Maryland, who was a member of that convention; he has opened such a scene of discord and accommodation of republicanism to despotism as must excite the most serious apprehensions in every patriotic mind.[1] The first argument has been noticed in the preceding essays; wherein it is shown that this is not the criterion whereby to determine the merits of the new constitution; that notwithstanding the reality of the distresses of the people, the new constitution may not only be inadequate as a remedy, but destructive of liberty, and the completion of misery. The remaining two arguments will be discussed in this number; their futility elucidated; and thus the medium of deception being dissipated, the public attention, with undirected, undiminished force, will be directed to the proper object, will be confined to the consideration of the nature and construction of the plan of government itself, the question will then be, whether this plan be calculated for our welfare, or misery; whether it is the temple of liberty, or the structure of despotism? and as the former, or the latter, shall appear to be the case, to adopt or reject it accordingly, otherwise to banish the demon of domination by suitable amendments and qualifications.

The evils of anarchy have been portrayed with all the imagery of language in the glowing colors of eloquence; the affrighted mind is thence led to clasp the new Constitution as the instrument of deliverance, as the only avenue to safety and happiness. To avoid the possible and transitory evils of one extreme, it is seduced into the certain and permanent misery necessarily attendant on the other. A state of anarchy from its very nature can never be of long continuance; the greater its violence the shorter the duration; order and security are immediately sought by the distracted people beneath the shelter of equal laws and the salutary restraints of regular government, and if this be not attainable absolute power is assumed by the *one*, or a *few*, who shall be the most enterprising and successful. If anarchy, therefore, were the inevitable consequence of rejecting the new Constitution, it would be infinitely better to incur it, for even then there would be at least the chance of a good government rising out of licentiousness; but to rush at once into despotism because there is a bare possibility of anarchy ensuing from the rejection, or from what is yet more visionary, the small delay that would be occasioned by a revision and correction of the proposed system of government is so superlatively weak, so fatally blind, that it is astonishing any person of common understanding should suffer such an imposition to have the least influence on his judgment; still more astonishing that so flimsy and deceptive a doctrine should make converts among the enlightened freemen of America, who have so long enjoyed the blessings of liberty; but when I view among such converts men otherwise *pre-eminent* it raises a blush for the weakness of humanity; that these, her brightest ornaments, should be so dimsighted to what is self-evident to most men, that such imbecility of judgment should appear where so much perfection was looked for; this ought to teach us to depend more on our own judgment and the nature of the case than upon the opinion of the greatest and best of men, who, from *constitutional* infirmities or *particular* situations, may sometimes view an object through a delusive medium, but the opinions of great men are more frequently the dictates of ambition or private interest.

The source of the apprehensions of this so much dreaded anarchy would upon investigation be found to arise from the artful suggestions of designing men, and not from a rational probability grounded on the actual state of affairs; the least reflection is sufficient to detect the fallacy to show that there is no one circumstance to justify the prediction of such an event. On the contrary a short time will evince, to the utter dismay and confusion of the conspirators, that a perseverance in cramming down their scheme of power upon the freemen of this State will inevitably produce *an anarchy* destructive of their darling domination, and *may* kindle a flame prejudicial to their safety; they should be cautious not to trespass too far on the forbearance of freemen when wresting their dearest concerns, but prudently retreat from the gathering storm.

The other specter that has been raised to terrify and alarm the people out of the exercise of their judgment on this great occasion, is the dread of our splitting into separate confederacies or republics, that might become rival powers and consequently liable to mutual wars from the usual motives of contention. This is an event still more improbable than the foregoing; it is a presumption unwarranted, either by the situation of affairs, or the sentiments of the people; no disposition leading to it exists; the advocates of the new constitution seem to view such a separation with horror, and its opponents are strenuously contending for a confederation that shall embrace all America under its comprehensive and salutary protection. This hobgoblin appears to have sprung from the deranged brain of *Publius*,[2] a New York writer, who, mistaking sound for argument, has with Herculean labor accumulated myriads of unmeaning sentences, and *mechanically* endeavored to force conviction by a torrent of misplaced words; he might have spared his readers the fatigue of wading through his long-winded disquisitions on the direful effects of the contentions of inimical states, as totally inapplicable to the subject he was *professedly* treating; this writer has devoted much time, and wasted more paper in combating chimeras of his own creation. However, for the sake of argument, I will admit that the necessary consequence of rejecting or delaying the establishment of the new constitution, would be the dissolution of the union, and the institution of even rival and inimical republics; yet ought such an apprehension, if well grounded, to drive us into the fangs of despotism? Infinitely preferable would be occasional wars to such an event; the former, although a severe scourge, is transient in its continuance, and in its operation partial, but a small proportion of the community are exposed to its greatest horrors, and yet fewer experience its greatest evils; the latter is permanent and universal misery, without remission or exemption: as passing clouds obscure for a time the splendor of the sun, so do wars interrupt the welfare of mankind; but despotism is a settled gloom that totally extinguishes happiness, not a ray of comfort can penetrate to cheer the dejected mind; the goad of power with unabating rigor insists upon the utmost exaction, like a merciless taskmaster, is continually inflicting the lash, and is never satiated with the feast of unfeeling domination, or the most abject servility.

The celebrated Lord Kaims,[3] whose disquisitions on human nature evidence extraordinary strength of judgment and depth of investigation, says that a continual *civil* war, which is the most destructive and horrible scene of human discord, is preferable to the uniformity of wretchedness and misery attendant upon despotism; of all *possible* evils, as I observed in my first number, *this* is the worst and the most to be *dreaded*.

I congratulate my fellow citizens that a good government, the greatest earthly blessing, may be so easily obtained, that our circumstances are so favorable, that nothing but the folly of the conspirators can produce anarchy or civil war, which would presently terminate in their destruction and the permanent harmony of the state, alone interrupted by their ambitious machinations.

In a former number I stated a charge of a very heinous nature, and highly prejudicial to the public welfare, and at this great crisis peculiarly alarming and threatening to liberty. I mean the suppression of the circulation of the newspapers from State to State by the of—c--rs of the P—t O—ce, who in violation of their duty and integrity, have prostituted their of—ces to forward the nefarious design of enslaving their countrymen, by thus cutting off all communication by the usual vehicle between the patriots of America; I find that notwithstanding that public appeal, they persevere in this villainous and daring practice. The newspapers of the other States that contain any useful information are still withheld from the printers of this State, and I see by the annunciation of the editor of Mr. Greenfeaf's patriotic New York paper, that the printers of that place are still treated in like manner. This informs his readers that but two southern papers have come to hand, and that they contain no information, which he affects to ascribe to the negligence of the p—t boy, not caring to quarrel with the p—t m—t—r g—l.

CENTINEL.

Philadelphia, January 12, 1788.

Centinel No. 12

To the PEOPLE OF PENNSYLVANIA. *Fellow Citizens.*

Conscious guilt has taken the alarm, thrown out the signal of distress, and even appealed to the generosity of patriotism. The authors and abettors of the new Constitution shudder at the term *conspirators* being applied to them, as it designates their true character, and seems prophetic of the catastrophe; they read their fate in the epithet.

In despair they are weakly endeavoring to screen their criminality by interposing the shield of the virtues of a Washington, in representing his concurrence in the proposed system of government as evidence of the purity of their intentions; but this impotent attempt to degrade the brightest ornament of his country to a base level with themselves will be considered as an aggravation of their treason, and an insult on the good sense of the people, who have too much discernment not to make a just discrimination between the honest mistaken zeal of the patriot and the flagitious machinations of an ambitious junto, and will resent the imposition that Machiavelian arts and consummate cunning have practiced upon our *illustrious chief.*

The term *conspirators* was not, as has been alleged, rashly or inconsiderately adopted; it is the language of dispassionate and deliberate reason, influenced by the purest patriotism; the consideration of the nature and construction of the new Constitution naturally suggests the epithet; its justness is strikingly illustrated by the conduct of the patrons of this plan of government, but if any doubt had remained whether this epithet is merited, it is now removed by the very uneasiness it occasions; this is a confirmation of its propriety. Innocence would have nothing to dread from such a stigma, but would triumph over the shafts of malice.

The conduct of men is the best clue to their principles. The system of deception that has been practiced; the constant solicitude shown to prevent information diffusing its salutary light are evidence of a conspiracy beyond the arts of sophistry to palliate, or the ingenuity of falsehood to invalidate; the means practiced to establish the new Constitution are demonstrative of the principles and designs of its authors and abettors.

At the time, says Mr. Martin (deputy from the State of Maryland in the general convention), when the public prints were announcing our perfect unanimity, discord prevailed to such a degree that the minority were upon the point of appealing to the public against the machinations of ambition. By such a base imposition, repeated in every newspaper and reverberated from one end of the union to the other, was the people lulled into a false confidence, into an implicit reliance upon the wisdom and patriotism of the convention; and when ambition, by her deceptive wiles, had succeeded to usher forth the new system of government with apparent unanimity of sentiment, the public delusion was complete. The most extravagant fictions were palmed upon the people, the seal of divinity was even ascribed to the new Constitution; a felicity more than human was to ensue from its establishment; overlooking the real cause of our difficulties and burthens, which have their proper remedy, the people were taught that the new Constitution would prove a mine of wealth and prosperity equal to every want, or the most sanguine desire; that it would effect what can only be produced by the exertion of industry and the practice of economy.

The conspirators, aware of the danger of delay, that allowing time for a rational investigation would prove fatal to their designs, precipitated the establishment of the new Constitution with all possible celerity; in Massachusetts the deputies of that convention, who are to give the final fiat in behalf of that great State to a measure upon which their dearest concerns depend, were elected by express in the first moments of blind enthusiasm; similar conduct has prevailed in the other States as far as circumstances permitted.

If the foregoing circumstances did not prove a conspiracy, there are others that must strike conviction in the most unsuspicious. Attempts to prevent discussion by shackling the press ought ever to be a signal of alarm to freemen, and considered as an annunciation of meditated tyranny; this is a truth that the uniform experience of mankind has established beyond the possibility of doubt. Bring the conduct of the authors and abettors of the new constitution to this test, let this be the criterion of their criminality, and every patriotic mind must unite in branding them with the stigma of conspirators against the public liberties. No stage of this business but what has been marked with every exertion of influence and device of ambition to suppress information and intimidate public discussion; the virtue and firmness of some of the printers rose superior to the menaces of violence and the lucre of private interest; when every means failed to shackle the press, the free and independent papers were attempted to be demolished by withdrawing all the subscriptions to them within the sphere of the influence of the conspirators; fortunately for the cause of liberty and truth, these daring high-handed attempts have failed except in one instance, where, from a peculiarity of circumstances, ambition has triumphed. Under the flimsy pretense of vindicating the character of a contemptible drudge of party, rendered ridiculous by his superlative folly in the late convention, of which the statement given in the Pennsylvania Herald was confessedly a faithful representation, this newspaper has been silenced by some hundreds of its subscribers (who it seems are generally among the devoted tools of party, or those who are obliged from their thraldom to yield implicit assent to the mandates of the junto) withdrawing their support from it; by this stroke the conspirators have suppressed the publication of the most valuable debates of the late convention, which would have been given in course by the editor of that paper, whose stipend now ceasing, he cannot afford without compensation the time and attention necessary to this business.

Every patriotic person who had an opportunity to hearing that illustrious advocate of liberty and his country, Mr. Findley,[1] must sensibly regret that his powerful arguments are not to extend beyond the confined walls of the State-House, where they could have so limited an effect; that the United States could not have been his auditory through the medium of the press. I anticipate the answer of the conspirators; they will tell you that this could not be their motive for silencing this paper, as the whole of the debates were taken down in short-hand by another person and published, but the public are not to be so easily duped, they will not receive a spurious as an equivalent for a genuine production; equal solicitude was expressed of the publication of the former as for the suppression of the latter—the public will judge of the motives.

That investigation into the nature and construction of the new constitution, which the conspirators have so long and zealously struggled against, has, notwithstanding their partial success, so far taken place as to ascertain the enormity of their criminality. That system which was pompously displayed as the perfection of government, proves upon examination to be the most odious system of tyranny that was ever projected, a many-headed hydra of despotism, whose complicated and various evils would be infinitely more oppressive and afflictive than the scourge of any single tyrant: the objects of dominion would be tortured to gratify the calls of ambition and the cravings of power of rival despots contending for the sceptre of superiority; the devoted people would experience a distraction of misery.

No wonder then that such a discovery should excite uneasy apprehensions in the minds of the conspirators, for such an attempt against the public liberties is unprecedented in history; it is a crime of the blackest dye, as it strikes at the happiness of millions and the dignity of human nature, as it was intended to deprive the inhabitants of so large a portion of the globe of the choicest blessings of life and the oppressed of all nations of an asylum.

The explicit language of the Centinel during the empire of delusion was not congenial to the feelings of the people, but truth when it has free scope is all powerful, it enforces conviction in the most prejudiced mind; he foresaw the consequences of an exertion of the good sense and understanding of the people, and predicted the defeat of the measure he ventured to attack, when it was deemed sacred by most men and the certain ruin of any who should dare to lisp a word against it: he has persevered through every discouraging appearance, and has now the satisfaction to find his countrymen are aware of their danger and are taking measures for their security.

Since writing the foregoing, I am informed that the printer of the Pennsylvania Herald is not quite decided whether he will drop his paper; he wishes, and perhaps will be enabled, to perseverve; however, the conspirators have effected their purpose; the editor is dismissed and the debates of the convention thereby suppressed.

CENTINEL.

To the PEOPLE OF PENNSYLVANIA. *Fellow Citizens.*

The conspirators are putting your good sense, patriotism and spirit to the severest test. So bold a game of deception, so decisive a stroke for despotic power, was never before attempted among enlightened freemen. Can there be apathy so indifferent as not to be roused into indignation, or prejudice so blind as not to yield to the glaring evidence of a flagitious conspiracy against the public liberties? The audacious and high-handed measures practiced to suppress information, and intimidate discussion, would in any other circumstances than the present, have kindled a flame fatal to such daring invaders of our dearest privileges.

The conspirators having been severely galled and checked in their career by the artillery of freedom, have made more vigorous and successful efforts to silence her batteries, while falsehood with all her delusions is making new and greater exertions in favor of ambition. On the one hand, every avenue to information is as far as possible cut off; the usual communication between the states, through the medium of the press, is in a great measure destroyed by a new arrangement at the Post Office—scarcely a newspaper is suffered to pass[1] by this conveyance, and the arguments of a Findley, a Whitehill and a Smilie, that bright constellation of patriots, are suppressed, and a spurious publication substituted; and on the other hand the select committee are assiduously employed in manufacturing deception in all its ensnaring colors, and having an adequate fund at their command, they are deluging the country with their productions. The only newspaper that circulates extensively out of the city is kept running over with deceptive inventions. Doctor Puff,[2] the paragraphist, has scarcely slept since his appointment, having received orders to work double tides; beneath his creative pen thousands of correspondents rise into view, who all harmonize in their sentiments and information about the new constitution; but the chief reliance is on James the Caledonian,[3] who can to appearance destroy all distinction between liberty and despotism, and make the latter pass for the former, who can bewilder truth in all the mazes of sophistry, and render the plainest propositions problematical. He, chameleon-like, can vary his appearance at pleasure, and assume any character for the purposes of deception. In the guise of a *Conciliator*, in the Independent Gazetteer, he professes great candor and moderation, admits some of the principal objections to the new constitution to be well founded and insidiously proposes a method to remove them, which is to consider the first Congress under the new constitution as a convention, competent to supply all defects in the system of government. This is really a discovery that does honor to his invention. What! a legislative declaration or law a basis upon which to rest our dearest liberties? Does he suppose the people have so little penetration as not to see through so flimsy a delusion, that such a security would amount to no more than the will and pleasure of their rulers, who might repeat this *fundamental* sanction whenever ambition stimulated? In the feigned *character* of *A Freeman*, he combats the weighty arguments of the minority of the late convention, by a mere play upon words, carefully avoiding the real merits of the question; and we moreover trace him in a variety of miscellaneous productions in every shape and form; he occasionally assists Doctor Puff in the fabrication of extracts of letters, paragraphs, correspondents, etc., etc.

So gifted and with such a claim of merit from his extraordinary and unwearied exertions in the cause of despotism, who so suitable or deserving of the office of Chief Justice of the United States? How congenial would such a post be to the principles and dispositions of James! Here he would be both judge and jury, sovereign arbiter in law and equity. In this capacity he may satiate his vengeance on patriotism for the opposition given to his projects of dominion. Here he may gratify his superlative arrogance and contempt of mankind, by trampling upon his fellow creatures with impunity, here he may give the finishing stroke to liberty, and silence the offensive complaints of violated justice and innocence, by adding the sanction of his office to the rapacity of power and the wantonness of oppression; there will be no intervening jury to shield the innocent, or procure redress to the injured. Fellow citizens, although the conspirators and their abettors are not sufficiently numerous to endanger our liberties by an open and forcible attack on them, yet when the characters of which they are composed and the methods they are practicing are considered, it ought to occasion the most serious alarm, and stimulate to an immediate, vigorous, and united exertion of the patriotic part of the community for the security of their rights and privileges. Societies ought to be instituted in every county, and a reciprocity of sentiments and information maintained between such societies, whereby the patriots throughout Pennsylvania, being mutually enlightened and invigorated, would form an invincible bulwark to liberty, and by unity of counsel, and exertion might the better procure and secure to themselves and to unborn ages the blessings of a good federal government. Nothing but such a system of conduct can frustrate the machinations of an ambitious junto, who, versed in Machiavellian arts can varnish over with the semblance of freedom the most despotic instrument of government ever projected; who cannot only veil over their own ambitious purposes, but raise an outcry against the real patriots for interested views, when they are advocating the cause of liberty and of their country by opposing a scheme of arbitrary power and office making; who can give the appearance of economy to the introduction of a numerous and permanent standing army, and the institution of lucrative, needless offices to provide for the swarms of gaping, almost famished expectants, who have been campaigning it for ten years without success against our inestimable State Constitution, as a reward for their persevering toils, but particularly for their zeal on the present occasion, and also as a phalanx to tyranny; and who, notwithstanding the testimony of uniform experience, evinces the necessity of restrictions on those entrusted with power, and a due dependence of the deputy on the constituent being maintained to ensure the public welfare; who, notwithstanding the fate that liberty has ever met from the remissness of the people and the persevering nature of ambition, who, ever on the watch, grasps at every avenue to supremacy. I say, notwithstanding such evidence before them of the folly of mankind, so often duped by similar arts, the conspirators have had the address to inculcate the opinion that forms of government are no security for the public liberties; that the administration is everything; that, although there would be no responsibility under the new Constitution—no restriction on the powers of the government, whose will and pleasure would be literally the law of the land, yet that we should be perfectly safe and happy. That as our rulers would be made of the same corrupt materials as ourselves, they certainly could not abuse the trust reposed in them, but would be the most self-denying order of beings ever created; with your purses at their absolute disposal, and your liberties at their discretion, they would be proof against the charms of money and the allurements of power. However, if such Utopian ideas should prove chimerical, and the people should find the yoke too heavy, they might at pleasure alleviate or even throw it off. In short, the conspirators have displayed so much ingenuity on this occasion, that if it had not been for the patriotism and firmness of some of the printers, which gave an opportunity to enlightened truth to come forward, and by her invincible powers to detect the sophistry and expose the fallacy of such impositions, liberty must have been overcome by the wiles of ambition, and this land of freemen have become the miserable abode of slaves.

CENTINEL.

Philadelphia, January 26, 1788

To the PEOPLE OF PENNSYLVANIA. *Fellow Citizens.*

I am happy to find the comment that I have made upon the nature and tendency of the new constitution, and my suspicions of the principles and designs of its authors, are fully confirmed by the evidence of the Honorable LUTHER MARTIN, esquire, late deputy in the general convention. He has laid open the conclave, exposed the dark scene within, developed the mystery of the proceedings, and illustrated the machinations of ambition. His public spirit has drawn upon him the rage of the conspirators, for daring to remove the veil of secrecy, and announcing to the public the meditated, gilded mischief: all their powers are exerting for his destruction, the mint of calumny is assiduously engaged in coining scandal to blacken his character, and thereby to invalidate his testimony; but this illustrious patriot will rise superior to all their low arts, and be the better confirmed in the good opinion and esteem of his fellow-citizens, upon whose gratitude he has an additional claim by standing forth their champion at a crisis when most men would have shrunk from such a duty. Mr. Martin has appealed to general Washington of the truth of what he has advanced, and undaunted by the threats of his and his country's enemies, is nobly persevering in the cause of liberty and mankind. I would earnestly recommend it to all well meaning persons to read his communication, as the most satisfactory and certain method of forming a just opinion on the present momentous question, particularly the three or four last continuances, as they go more upon the general principles and tendency of the new constitution. I have in former numbers alluded to some passages in this publication; I shall in this number quote some few others, referring to the work itself for a more lengthy detail. The following paragraphs are extracted from the continuances republished in the "Independent Gazetteer" of the 25th January, and the "Pennsylvania Packet" of the 1st February instant, viz.

"By the eighth section of this article, Congress is to have power to lay and collect taxes, duties, imposts, and excises. When we met in convention after our adjournment, to receive the report of the committee of detail, the members of that committee were requested to inform us what powers were meant to be vested in Congress by the word duties in this section, since the word imposts extended to duties on goods imported, and by another part of the system no duties on exports were to be laid. In answer to this inquiry we were informed, that it was meant to give the general government the power of laying stamp duties on paper, parchment and vellum. We then proposed to have the power inserted in express words, lest disputes hereafter might arise on the subject, and that the meaning might be understood by all who were to be affected by it; but to this it was objected, because it was said that the word stamp would probably sound odiously in the ears of many of the inhabitants, and be a cause of objection. By the power of imposing stamp duties the Congress will have a right to declare that no wills, deeds, or other instruments of writing, shall be good and valid, without being stamped—that without being reduced to writing and being stamped, no bargain, sale, transfer of property or contract of any kind or nature whatsoever shall be binding; and also that no exemplifications of records, depositions, or probatees of any kind shall be received in evidence, unless they have the same solemnity. They may likewise oblige all proceedings of a judicial nature to be stamped to give them effect—those stamp duties may be imposed to any amount they please—and under the pretense of se-curing the collection of these duties, and to prevent the laws which imposed them from being evaded, the Congress may bring the deci-sion of all questions relating to the conveyance, disposition and rights of property, and every question relating to contract between man and man, into the courts of the general government—their inferior courts in the first instance and the superior court by appeal. By the power to lay and collect imposts, they may impose duties on any or every ar-ticle of commerce imported into these states, to what amount they please. By the power to lay excises, a power very odious in its nature, since it authorizes officers to go into your houses, your kitchens, your cellars, and to examine into your private concerns, the Congress may impose duties on every article of use or consumption; on the food that we eat—on the liquors we drink—on the clothes we wear—on the glass which enlightens our houses—on the hearths necessary for our warmth and comfort. By the power to lay and collect taxes, they may proceed to direct taxation on every individual, either by a capi-tation tax on their heads, or an assessment on their property. By this part of the section, therefore, the government has a power to lay what duties they please afterwards on whatever we use or consume—to impose stamp duties to what amount they please, and in whatever cases they please—afterwards to impose on the people direct taxes, by capitation tax, or by assessment, to what amount they choose, and thus to sluice them at every vein as long as they have a drop of blood, without any control, limitation or restraint—while all the officers for collecting these taxes, stamp duties, imposts and excises, are to be appointed by the general government, under its direction, not accountable to the states; nor is there even a security that they shall be citizens of the respective states, in which they are to exercise their offices; at the same time the construction of every law imposing any and all these taxes and duties, and directing the collection of them, and every question arising thereon, and on the conduct of the officers appointed to execute these laws, and to collect these taxes and duties so various in their kinds, are taken away from the courts of justice of the different states, and confined to the courts of the general government, there to be heard and determined by judges holding their offices under the appointment, not of the states, but of the general government.

"Many of the members, and myself in the number, thought that the states were much better judges of the circumstances of their citizens, and what sum of money could be collected from them by direct taxation, and of the manner in which it could be raised with the greatest ease and convenience to their citizens, than the general government could be; and that the general government ought not in any case to have the power of laying direct taxes, but in that of the delinquency of a state. Agreeable to this sentiment, I brought in a proposition on which a vote of the convention was taken. The proposition was as follows: 'And whenever the legislature of the United States shall find it necessary that revenue should be raised by direct taxation, having appointed the same by the above rule, requisitions shall be made of the respective states to pay into the continental treasury their respective quotas within a time in the said requisition to be specified, and in case of any of the states failing to comply with such requisition, then and then only, to have power to devise and pass acts directing the mode and authorizing the collection of the same.' Had this proposition been acceded to, the dangerous and oppressive power in the general government of imposing direct taxes on the inhabitants, which it now enjoys in all cases, would have been only vested in it in case of the non-compliance of a state, as a punishment for its delinquency, and would have ceased that moment that the state complied with the requisition. But the proposition was rejected by a majority, consistent with their aim and desire of increasing the power of the general government as far as possible, and destroying the power and influence of the states. And though there is a provision that all duties, imposts and excises shall be uniform, that is, to be laid to the same amount on the same articles in each state, yet this will not prevent Congress from having it in their power to cause them to fall very unequal and much heavier on some states than on others, because these duties may be laid on articles but little or not at all used in some states, and of absolute necessity for the use and consumption of others, in which case the first would pay little or no part of the revenue arising therefrom, while the whole or nearly the whole of it would be paid by the last, to wit: The states which use and consume the articles on which the imposts and excises are laid."

Another extract, viz:

"But even this provision, apparently for the security of the State governments, inadequate as it is, is entirely left at the mercy of the general government, for by the fourth section of the first article, it is expressly provided, that the Congress shall have a power to make and alter all regulations concerning the time and manner of holding elections for senators—a provision expressly looking forward to, and I have no doubt designed for the utter extinction and abolition of all State governments. Nor will this, I believe, be doubted by any person, when I inform you that some of the warm advocates and patrons of the system in convention, strenuously opposed the choice of the senators by the State legislatures, insisting that the State governments ought not to be introduced in any manner so as to be component parts of or instruments for, carrying into execution the general government. Nay, so far were the friends of the system from pretending that they mean it or considered it as a federal system, that on the question being proposed, 'that a union of the States merely federal ought to be the sole object of the exercise of the powers vested in the convention,' it was negatived by a majority of the members, and it was resolved that a national government ought to be formed.' Afterwards the word 'national' was struck out by them, because they thought the word might tend to alarm; and although now they who advocate the system pretend to call themselves federalists, in convention the distinction was just the reverse: those who opposed the system, were there considered and styled the federal party; those who advocated it, the anti-federal.

"Viewing it as a national, not a federal government; as calculated and designed not to protect and preserve, but to abolish and annihilate the State governments, it was opposed for the following reasons:—It was said that this continent was much too extensive for one national government, which should have sufficient power and energy to pervade and hold in obedience and subjection all its parts, consistent with the enjoyment and preservation of liberty; that the genius and habits of the people of America were opposed to such a government; that during their connection with Great Britain, they had been accustomed to have all their concerns transacted within a narrow circle—their colonial districts; they had been accustomed to have their seats of government near them, to which they might have access without much inconvenience, when their business should require it; that at this time we find if a county is rather large, the people complain of the inconvenience, and clamor for a division of their county, or for a removal of the place where their courts are held, so as to render it more central and convenient; that in those States, the territory of which is extensive, as soon as the population increases remote from the seat of government, the inhabitants are urgent for a removal of the seat of their government, or to be erected into a new state. As a proof of this, the inhabitants of the western parts of Virginia and North Carolina, of Vermont and the province of Maine, were instances; even the inhabitants of the western parts of Pennsylvania, who it was said already seriously look forward to the time when they shall either be erected into a new State, or have their seat of government removed to the Susquehanna. If the inhabitants of the different States consider it as a grievance to attend a county court, or the seat of their own government, when a little inconvenient, can it be supposed they would ever submit to have a national government established, the seat of which would be more than a thousand miles removed from some of them? It was insisted that governments of a republican nature are those best calculated to preserve the freedom and happiness of the citizen; that governments of this kind are only calculated for a territory but small in its extent; that the only method by which an extensive continent like America could be connected and united together consistent with the principles of freedom, must be by having a number of strong and energetic state governments for securing and protecting the rights of the individuals forming those governments, and for regulating all their concerns, and a strong, energetic federal government over those states for the protection and preservation, and for regulating the common concerns of the States; it was further insisted, that even if it was possible to effect a total abolition of the State governments at this time, and to establish one general government over the people of America, it could not long subsist, but in a little time would again be broken into a variety of governments of a smaller extent, similar in some manner to the present situation of this continent: the principal difference in all probability would be that the governments, so established, being effected by some violent convulsions, might not be formed on principles so favorable to liberty as those of our present State governments; that this ought to be an important consideration to such of the states who had excellent governments, which was the case with Maryland and most others, whatever it might be to persons who, disapproving of their particular state government, would be willing to hazard everything to overturn and destroy it. These reasons, sir, influenced me to vote against two branches in the legislature, and against every part of the system which was repugnant to the principles of a federal government. Nor was there a single argument urged, or reason assigned, which to my mind was satisfactory, to prove that a good government on federal principles was unattainable—the whole of their arguments only proving, what none of us controverted, that our federal government as originally formed was defective, and wanted amendment. However, a majority of the convention hastily and inconsiderately, without condescending to make a fair trial, in their great wisdom, decided that a kind of government which a Montesquieu and a Price have declared the best calculated of any to preserve internal liberty, and to enjoy external strength and security, and the only one by which a large continent can be connected and united consistent with the principles of liberty, was totally impracticable, and they acted accordingly."

After such information, what are we to think of the declarations of Mr. Wilson, who assured our state convention that it was neither the intention of the authors of the new constitution, nor its tendency, to establish a consolidated or national government, founded upon the destruction of the State governments, that such could not have been the design of the general convention he said was certain, because the testimony of experience, the opinions of the most celebrated writers, and the nature of the case demonstrated in the clearest manner that so extensive a territory as these United States include could not be governed by any other mode than a confederacy of republics consistent with the principles of freedom, and that their own conviction was that nothing short of the supremacy of despotism could connect and bind together this country under ONE GOVERNMENT? Has any one a doubt now remaining of the guilt of the conspirators!

The O—rs of the P—t O—ce, fearful of the consequences of their conduct, are taking measures to invalidate the charge made against them. As this is a matter of the highest importance to the public, it will be necessary to state the charge and the evidence. In two of my former numbers, I asserted that the patriotic newspapers of this city and that of New York miscarried in their passage, whilst the vehicles of despotism, meaning those newspapers in favor of the new constitution, passed as usual; and it was particularly asserted that the patriotic essays of Brutus, Cincinnatus, Cato, etc., published at New York, were withheld during the greatest part of the time that our state convention sat; and in a late number, I further asserted that since the late arrangement at the P—t O—ce, scarcely a newspaper was suffered to pass by the usual conveyance, and of the truth of this last charge I appealed to the printers; however, I understand this last is not denied or controverted. When the dependence of the printers on the P—t O—ce is considered, the injury they may sustain by incurring the displeasure of these of—rs, and when to this is added that of the complexion of the printers in respect to the new constitution, that most of them are zealous in prompting its advancement, it can scarcely be expected that they would volunteer it against the P—t O—rs, or refuse their names to a certificate that the newspapers arrived as usual prior to the first of January, when the new arrangement took place; however, the printer of the Freeman's Journal when applied to, had the spirit to refuse his name to the establishment of a falsehood, and upon being called upon to specify the missing papers, particularly during the sitting of the State convention, he pointed out and offered to give a list of a considerable number, instancing no less than seven successive Greenleaf's patriotic New York papers, besides others occasionally withheld from him; Colonel Oswald was out of town when his family was applied to, or, I have no doubt, he would have observed a similar conduct. But there is a fact that will invalidate any certificate that can be procured on this occasion, and is alone demonstrative of the suppression of the patriotic newspapers. The opponents to the new constitution in this state were anxious to avail themselves of the well-written essays of the New York patriots, such as Brutus, Cincinnatus, Cato, etc. and with that view were attentive to have them republished here as soon as they came to hand, and especially during the sitting of our state convention, when they would have been the most useful to the cause of liberty by operating on the members of that convention; a recurrence to the free papers of this city at that period, will show a great chasm in these republications, owing to the miscarriage of Greenleaf's New York papers. Agreeable to my assertions it will appear that for the greatest part of the time that our state convention sat, scarcely any of the number of Brutus, Cincinnatus, Cato, etc., were republished in this city; the fifth number of Cincinnatus, that contained very material information about the finances of the union, which strikes at some of the principal arguments in favor of the new constitution, which was published at New York the 29th November, was not republished here until the 15th December following, two or three days after the convention rose, and so of most of the other numbers of this and the other signatures; so great was the desire of the opponents here to republish them, that the fourth number of Cincinnatus was republished so lately as in Mr. Bailey's last paper, which with other missing numbers were procured by private hands from New York, and in two or three instances, irregular numbers were republished. The new arrangement at the P—t O—ce, novel in its nature, and peculiarly injurious by the suppression of information at this great crisis of public affairs, is a circumstance highly presumptive of the truth of the other charge.

CENTINEL.

CENTINEL NO. 15

To the PEOPLE OF PENNSYLVANIA. *Fellow Citizens.*

There are few of the maxims or opinions we hold, that are the result of our own investigation or observation, and even those we adopt from others are seldom on a conviction of their truth or propriety, but from the fascination of example and the influence of what is or appears to be the general sentiment. The science of government being the most abstruse and unobvious of all others, mankind are more liable to be imposed upon by the artful and designing in systems and regulations of government, than on any other subject: hence a jealousy of innovation confirmed by uniform experience prevails in most communities; this reluctance to change has been found to be the greatest security of free governments, and the principal bulwark of liberty; for the aspiring and ever-restless spirit of ambition would otherwise, by her deceptive wiles and ensnaring glosses, triumph over the freest and most enlightened people. It is the peculiar misfortune of the people of these United States, at this awful crisis of public affairs, to have lost this useful, this absolutely necessary jealousy of innovation in government, and thereby to lie at the mercy and be exposed to all the artifices of ambition, without this usual shield to protect them from imposition. The conspirators, well aware of their advantage, have seized the favorable moment, and by the most unparalleled arts of deception, have obtained the sanction of the conventions of several states to the most tyranic system of government ever projected.

The magic of great names, the delusion of falsehood, the suppression of information, precipitation and fraud have been the instruments of this partial success, the pillars whereon the structure of tyranny has been so far raised. Those influential vehicles, the newspapers, with few exceptions, have been devoted to the cause of despotism, and by the subserviency of the P— O—, the usefulness of the patriotic newspapers has been confined to the places of their publication, whilst falsehood and deception have had universal circulation, without the opportunity of refutation. The feigned unanimity of one part of America, has been represented to produce the acquiescence of another, and so mutually to impose upon the whole by the force of example.

The adoption of the new constitution by the convention of the state of Massachusetts, by a majority of nineteen out of near four

90

hundred members, and that too qualified by a number of propositions of amendment, cannot afford the conspirators much cause for triumph, and especially when all the circumstances under which it has been obtained are considered. The late alarming disorders which distracted that state, and even threatened subversion of all order and government, and were with difficulty suppressed, occasioned the greatest consternation among all men of property and rank.[1] In this disposition even the most high-toned and arbitrary government became desirable as a security against licentiousness and agrarian laws; consequently the new constitution was embraced with eagerness by men of these descriptions, who in every community form a powerful interest, and, added to the conspirators, office hunters, etc., etc., made a formidable and numerous party in favor of the new constitution. The elections of the members of convention were, moreover, made in the first moments of blind enthusiasm, when every artifice was practiced to prejudice the people against all those who had the enlightened patriotism to oppose this system of tyranny. Thus was almost every man of real ability, who was in opposition, excluded from a seat in this convention. Consequently the contest was very unequal: well-meaning though uninformed men were opposed to great learning, eloquence, and sophistry, in the shape of lawyers, doctors, and divines, who were capable and seemed disposed to delude by deceptive glosses and specious reasoning. Indeed, from the specimens we have seen of the discussion on this occasion, every enlightened patriot must regret that the cause of liberty has been so weakly although zealously advocated—that its champions were so little illuminated. In addition to these numerous advantages in the convention, the friends of the new constitution had the weight and influence of the town of Boston to second their endeavors, and yet, notwithstanding all this, were near losing the question, although delusively qualified. Is this any evidence of the excellency of the new constitution? Certainly not. Nor can it have any influence in inducing the remaining states to accede. They will examine and judge for themselves, and from their wisdom in taking due time for deliberation, I have no doubt will prove the salvation of the liberties of the United States.

CENTINEL.

Philadelphia, February 20th, 1788.

CENTINEL No. 16

To the PEOPLE OF PENNSYLVANIA. *Fellow Citizens.*

The new constitution, instead of being the panacea or cure of every grievance so delusively represented by its advocates, will be found upon examination like Pandora's box, replete with every evil. The most specious clauses of this system of ambition and iniquity contain latent mischief, and premeditated villainy. By section 9th of the Ist article, "No *ex post facto* law shall be passed." This sounds very well upon a superficial consideration, and I dare say has been read by most people with approbation. Government undoubtedly ought to avoid retrospective laws as far as may be, as they are generally injurious and fraudulent: yet there are occasions when such laws are not only just but highly requisite. An ex post facto law is a law made after the fact, so that the Congress under the new constitution are precluded from all control over transactions prior to its establishment. This prohibition would screen the numerous public defaulters, as no measure could be constitutionally taken to compel them to render an account and restore the public moneys; the unaccounted millions lying in their hands would become their private property. Hitherto these characters from their great weight and numbers have had the influence to prevent an investigation of their accounts; but if this constitution be established, they may set the public at defiance, as they would be completely exonerated of all demands of the United States against them. This is not a strained construction of this section, but the proper evident meaning of the words, which not even the ingenuity or sophistry of the *Caledonian*[1] can disguise from the meanest capacity. However if this matter admitted of any doubt, it would be removed by the following consideration, viz., that the new constitution is founded upon a dissolution of the present articles of confederation and is an original compact between those states, or rather those individuals, who accede to it; consequently all contracts, debts and engagements in favor or against the United States, under the *old* government, are cancelled unless they are provided for in the *new* constitution. The framers of this constitution appear to have been aware of such consequence by stipulating in article 6th, that all debts contracted, and engagements entered into before the adoption of this constitution shall be valid *against* the United States under the new constitution, but there is no provision that the debts, etc., due *to* the

United States, shall be valid or recoverable. This is a striking omission, and must have been designed, as debts of the latter description would naturally occur and claim equal attention with the former. This article implied, cancels all debts due to the United States prior to the establishment of the new Constitution. If equal provision had been made for the debts due *to* the United States, as *against* the United States, the ex post facto clause would not have so pernicious an operation.

The immaculate convention that is said to have possessed the fullness of patriotism, wisdom and virtue, contained a number of the principal public defaulters; and these were the most influential members and chiefly instrumental in the framing of the new constitution. There were several of this description in the deputation from the state of Pennsylvania, who have long standing and immense accounts to settle, and MILLIONS perhaps to refund. The late Financier[2] alone, in the capacity of chairman of the commercial committee of Congress, early in the late war, was entrusted with millions of public money, which to this day remain unaccounted for, nor has he settled his accounts as Financier. The others may also find it a convenient method to balance accounts with the public; they are sufficiently known and therefore need not be designated. This will account for the zealous attachment of such characters to the new constitution and their dread of investigation and discussion. It may be said that the new Congress would rather break through the constitution than suffer the public to be defrauded of so much treasure, when the burthens and distresses of the people are so very great; but this is not to be expected from the characters of which that Congress would in all probability be composed, if we may judge from the predominant influence and interest these defaulters now possess in many of the states. Besides, should Congress be disposed to violate the fundamental articles of the constitution for the sake of public justice, they would be prevented in so doing by their oaths,[3] but even if this should not prove an obstacle, if it can be supposed that any set of men would perjure themselves for the public good, and combat an host of enemies on such terms, still it would be of no avail, as there is a further barrier interposed between the public and these defaulters, namely, the supreme court of the union, whose province it would be to determine the constitutionality of any law that may be controverted; and supposing no bribery or corrupt influence practiced on the bench of judges, it would be their sworn duty to refuse their sanction to laws made in the face and contrary to the letter and spirit of the constitution, as any law to compel the settlement of accounts and payment of moneys depending and due under the old confederation would be. The Ist section of 3d article gives the supreme court cognizance of not only the laws, but of all cases arising under the constitution, which empowers this tribunal to decide upon the construction of the constitution itself in the last resort. This is so extraordinary, so unprecedented, an authority that the intention in vesting of it must have been to put it out of the power of Congress, even by breaking through the constitution, to compel these defaulters to restore the public treasure.

In the present circumstances these sections of the new constitution would be also productive of great injustice between the respective states; the delinquent states would be exonerated from all existing demands against them on account of the great arrearages of former requisitions, as they could not be constitutionally compelled to discharge them. And as the majority of the states are in this predicament, and have an equal voice in the senate, it would be their interest, and in their power by not only the constitution, but by a superiority of votes, to prevent the levying of such arrearages. Besides the constitution, moreover, declares that all taxes, etc. shall be uniform throughout the United States, which is an additional obstacle against noticing them.

The state of Pennsylvania in such cases would have no credit for her extraordinary exertions and punctuality heretofore; but would be taxed equally with those states which for years past have not contributed anything to the common expenses of the union; indeed, some of the states have paid nothing since the revolution.

CENTINEL.

Philadelphia, 23d February, 1788.

CENTINEL NO. 17

To the PEOPLE OF PENNSYLVANIA. *Fellow Citizens.*

In my last number I exposed the villainous intention of the framers of the new constitution, to defraud the public out of the millions lying in the hands of individuals by the construction of this system, which would, if established, cancel all debts now due to the United States. I also showed that thereby the delinquent states would be exonerated of all arrearages due by them on former requisitions of Congress; and to prove that the cancelling of all public dues was premeditated in regard to individuals, I stated that the general convention contained a number of the principal public defaulters, and that these were the most influential members, and chiefly instrumental in framing the new constitution: in answer to which, the conspirators have, by bold assertions, spurious vouchers, and insufficient certificates, endeavored to exculpate one member, and to alleviate the weight of the charge of delinquency against another. In the face of a resolution of Congress of the 20th June, 1785, declaring their intention of appointing three commissioners, to settle and adjust the receipts and expenditures of the late financier, the conspirators have asserted that his accounts were finally settled in November, 1784, for which they pretend to have vouchers, and by a pompous display of certain resolutions of Congress, respecting a particular charge of fraud against him, as commercial agent to the United States, they vainly hope to divert the public attention from his great delinquency, in never accounting for the millions of public money entrusted to him in that line. When we consider the immense sums of money taken up by Mr. M—s,[1] as commercial agent, to import military supplies, and even to trade in behalf of the United States, at a time when the risk was so great, that individuals would not venture their property; that all these transactions were conducted under the private firm of W—g and M—,[2] which afforded unrestrained scope to speculation and embezzlement of the public property, by enabling Mr. M—s to throw the loss of all captures by the enemy, at that hazardous period, on the public, and converting most of the safe arrivals (which were consequently very valuable) into his private property; and when we add to these considerations the principles of the MAN, his bankrupt situation at the commencement of the late war, and the immense wealth he has dazzled the world with since, can it be thought unreasonable to conclude, that

95

the principal source of his affluence was the commercial agency of the United States, during the war?—not that I would derogate from his successful ingenuity in his numerous speculations in the paper moneys, Havannah monopoly and job, or in the sphere of financiering.

The certificate published in behalf of general M-ffl-n,[3] the quartermaster gen—l, will not satisfy a discerning public, or acquit him of the charge of delinquency, as this certificate was procured to serve an electioneering purpose, upon a superficial and hasty inspection of his general account, unchecked by the accounts of his deputies, whose receipts and expenditures had not been examined, and consequently, by errors, collusion between him and them, or otherwise g—l M-ffl-n may retain a large balance in his hands; in such case a *quietus* may have been thought expedient to continue his affluence.

For the honor of human nature, I wish to draw a veil over the situation and conduct of another weighty character, whose name has given a false lustre to the new constitution, and been the occasion of sullying the laurels of a *Washington* by inducing him to acquiesce in a system of despotism and villainy, at which enlightened patriotism shudders.

The discovery of the intended fraud, which for magnitude and audacity is unparalleled, must open the eyes of the deluded to the true character and principles of the men who had assumed the garb of patriotism with an insidious design of enslaving and robbing their fellow citizens, of establishing those odious distinctions between the well-born and the great body of the people, of degrading the latter to the level of slaves and elevating the former to the rank of nobility.

The citizens of this state, which is in advance in its payments to the federal treasury, whilst some of the others have not paid a farthing since the war, ought in a peculiar manner to resent the intended imposition and make its authors experience their just resentment; it is incumbent upon them in a particular manner to exert themselves to frustrate the measures of the conspirators, and set an example to those parts of the union who have not enjoyed the blessing of a free press on this occasion, but are still enveloped in the darkness of delusion, and enthralled by the fascination of names.

Could it have been supposed seven years ago, that, before the wounds received in the late conflict for liberty were scarcely healed, a postmaster-general and his deputies would have had the daring pre-

sumption to convert an establishment intended to promote and secure the public welfare into an engine of despotism, by suppressing
all those newspapers that contain the essays of patriotism and real
intelligence, and propagating instead thereof falsehoods and delusion? Such a supposition at that time would have been treated as
chimerical; but how must our indignation rise when we find this flagitious practice is persevered in, after being publicly detected! Must
not the bribe from the conspirators be very great to compensate the
postmaster-general and his deputies for the loss of character and infamy consequent upon such conduct, and for the danger they incur of
being impeached and turned out of office?

The scurrilous attack of the *little Fiddler*[4] upon Mr. Workman of
the university, on a suspicion, perhaps unfounded, of his being the
author of a series of essays under the signature of *Philadelphiensis*,
is characteristic of the man. He has ever been the base parasite and
tool of the wealthy and great, at the expense of truth, honor, friend-
ship, treachery to benefactors—nay, to the nearest relatives: all have
been sacrificed by him at the shrine of the great. He ought, however,
to have avoided a contrast with so worthy and highly respected a
character as Mr. Workman, who had an equal right with himself to
offer his sentiments on the new constitution; and if he viewed it as a
system of despotism, and had talents to unfold its nature and tendency, he deserves the thanks of every patriotic American, if he has
exerted them under the character of Philadelphiensis. His not being
above four years in the country can be no objection. The celebrated
Thomas Paine wrote his Common Sense before he had been two years
in America, which was not the less useful or acceptable upon that
account. The public have nothing to do with the author of a piece: it
is the merits of the writing that are alone to be considered. Mr. Workman, prior to his coming to America, was a professor in an eminent
academy in Dublin. Little Francis should have been cautious in giving provocation, for insignificance alone could have preserved him
the smallest remnant of character. I hope he will take the hint, or such
a scene will be laid open as will disgrace even his patrons; the suit of
clothes, and the quarter cask of wine, will not be forgot.

CENTINEL.

Philadelphia, March 19th, 1788.

To the PEOPLE OF PENNSYLVANIA. *Fellow Citizens.*

The measures that are pursuing to effect the establishment of the new constitution, are so repugnant to truth, honor, and the well-being of society, as would disgrace any cause. If the nature and tendency of this system were to be judged of by the conduct of its framers and patrons, what a picture of ambition and villainy would present itself to our view! From the specimens they have already given, anticipation may easily realize the consequences that would flow from the new constitution, if established; we may bid adieu to all the blessings of liberty, to all the fruits of the late glorious assertion of the rights of human nature, made at the expense of so much blood and treasure. Yet such is the infatuation of many well meaning persons, that they view with indifference the atrocious villainy which characterizes the proceedings of the advocates of the new system. The daring, and in most parts of the United States, the successful methods practised to shackle the press, and destroy the freedom of discussion, the silencing the Pennsylvania Herald, to prevent the publication of the invaluable debates of the late convention of this state; the total suppression of real intelligence, and of the illuminations of patriotism, through the medium of the post-office; the systematic fraud and deception that pervade the union; the stigmatizing, and by every art which ambition and malice can suggest, laboring to vilify, intimidate and trample under foot every disinterested patriot who, preferring his country's good to every other consideration, has the courage to stand forth the champion of liberty and the people; and the intercepting of private confidential letters passing from man to man, violating the sacredness of a seal and thus infringing one of the first privileges of freemen—that of communicating with each other[1]: I say all these are overlooked by the infatuated admirers of the new system, who, deluded by the *phantom* of wealth and prosperity, profit not by the admonitory lesson which such proceedings afford, are deaf to the calls of patriotism, and would rush blindly into the noose of ambition.

However, to the honor of Pennsylvania, a very large majority of her citizens view the subject in its true light, and spurn the shackles prepared for them. They will in due time convince the aspiring despots and avaricious office-hunters, that their dark intrigues, and deep concerted schemes of power and aggrandizement, are ineffectual; that they are neither to be duped nor dragooned out of their liberties. The conspirators, I know, insolently boast that their strength in the other states will enable them to crush the opposition in this; but let them not build upon that which is in its nature precarious and transient, which must fail them the moment the delusion is dispelled. Their success in the other states is the fruit of deceptions that cannot be long supported. Indeed, the audacity and villainy of the conspirators on the one hand, and the frantic enthusiasm and easy credulity of the people on the other, in some of the states, however well attested and recorded in the faithful page of history, will be treated by posterity as fabulous.

The great artifice that is played off on this occasion, is the persuading the people of one place, that the people everywhere else are nearly unanimous in favor of the new system, and thus endeavoring by the fascination of example and force of general opinion to prevail upon the people every where to acquiesce in what is represented to them as the general sentiment.

Thus as one means of deception has failed them, they have adopted another, always avoiding rational discussion. When the glare of great names, the dread of annihilation if the new system was rejected or the adoption of it even delayed, were dissipated by the artillery of truth and reason; they have recurred to the one now practising, the intimidating and imposing influence of imaginary numbers and unanimity that are continually reverberated from every part of the union, by the tools and vehicles of the would-be despots; and in which they have had astonishing success. The people in the Eastern States have been taught to believe that it is all harmony to the Southward; and in the Southern States they are discouraged from opposition by the unanimity of the Eastern and Northern States; nay, what will appear incredible, considering the distance, a gentleman of veracity just returned from New York, assures that the conspirators have had the address to inculcate an opinion there that all opposition had ceased in this state, notwithstanding the evidence of the contrary is so glaring here; this gentleman further informs, that so entirely devoted is the post-office, that not a single newspaper is received by the printers of that place from this city or elsewhere; and a Boston newspaper, come by private hand, announces to the public, that for some months past, the printers there have received no newspapers to the Southward of New Haven, in Connecticut, where the press is muzzled, and consequently cannot injure the cause; that all intelligence of the occurrences in the other States is withheld from them; and that they know more of the state of Europe, than of their own country.

Notwithstanding many thousand copies of the Reasons of Dissent of the minority of the late convention of this state were printed and forwarded in every direction, and by various conveyances, scarcely any of these got beyond the limits of this state, and most of them not until a long time after their publication.[2] The printer of these Reasons, by particular desire, addressed a copy of them to every printer in the union, which he sent to the Post Office to be conveyed in the mail as usual, long before the *new arrangement*, as it is called, took place; and yet we since find that none of them reached the place of their destination. This is a full demonstration of the subserviency of the Post Office, and a striking evidence of the vigilance that has been exerted to suppress information. It is greatly to be regretted that the opposition in Massachusetts were denied the benefits of our discussion that the unanswerable dissent of our minority did not reach Boston in time to influence the decision of the great question by their convention as it would in all probability have enabled patriotism to triumph; not that I would derogate from the good sense and public spirit of that state, which I have no doubt would in common circumstances have shone with equal splendor, but this was far from being the case; the new constitution was viewed in Massachusetts through the medium of a SHAYS, the terrors of HIS insurrection had not subsided; a government that would have been execrated at another time was embraced by many as a refuge from anarchy, and thus liberty deformed by mad riot and dissention, lost her ablest advocates.[3]

As the liberties of all the states in the union are struck at in common with those of Pennsylvania, by the conduct of the Post Master General and deputies, I trust that the example which her Legislature[4] has set by instructing her delegates in Congress on this subject, will be followed by the others, that with one accord they will hurl their vengeance on the venal instruments of ambition, who have presumed to prostrate one of the principal bulwarks of liberty. In a confederated government of such extent as the United States, the freest communication of sentiment and information should be maintained, as the liberties, happiness and welfare of the union depend upon a concert of counsels; the signals of alarm whenever ambition should rear its baneful head, ought to be uniform. Without this communication between the members of the confederacy the freedom of the press, if it could be maintained in so severed a situation, would cease to be a security against the encroachments of tyranny. The truth of the foregoing position is strikingly illustrated on the present occasion; for want of this intercommunity of sentiment and information, the liberties of this country are brought to an awful crisis; ambition has made a great stride towards dominion, has succeeded through the medium of muzzled presses to delude a great body of the people in the other states, and threatens to overwhelm the enlightened opposition in this by *external* force. Here, indeed, notwithstanding every nerve was strained by the conspirators, to muzzle or demolish every newspaper that allowed free discussion, two printers have asserted the independency of the press, whereby the arts of ambition have been detected, and the new system has been portrayed in its native villainy; its advocates have long since abandoned the field of argument, relinquished the unequal contest, and truth and patriotism reign triumphant in this state; but the conspirators trust to their success in the other states for the attainment of their darling object, and therefore all their vigilance is exerted to prevent the infectious spirit of freedom and enlightened patriotism communicating to the rest of the union—all intercourse is as far as possible cut off.

To rectify the erroneous representation made in the other states of the sentiments of the people in this respecting the new constitution, I think it my duty to state the fact as it really is.—Those who favor this system of tyranny are most numerous in the city of Philadelphia, where perhaps they may be a considerable majority. In the most eastern counties they compose about one-fourth of the people, but in the middle, northern and western counties not above a twentieth part, so that upon the whole the friends to the new constitution in this state are about one-sixth of the people. The following circumstance is an evidence of the spirit and decision of the opposition.—An individual, unadvisedly and without concert, and contrary to the system of conduct generally agreed upon, went to the expense of printing and circulating an address to the legislature, reprobating in the strongest terms the new constitution, and praying that the deputies of this state in the federal convention, who in violation of their duty acceded to the new constitution, be called to account for their daring procedure. This address, or petition, was signed by upwards of four thousand citizens in only two counties, viz., Franklin and Cumberland; and if the time had admitted, prior to the adjournment of the legislature, there is reason to believe that this high-toned application would have been subscribed by five-sixth of the freemen of this state. The advocates of the new constitution, availing themselves of this partial measure of two counties, have asserted it to be the result of a general exertion, which is so evidently false that it can only deceive people at a distance from us, for the counties over the mountain are nearly unanimous in the opposition. In Fayette at a numerous county meeting, there appeared to be but two persons in favor of the constitution; in Bedford county, in the mountains, there are not above twenty; in Huntingdon adjoining, about 30; in Dauphin, in the middle country, not 100; in Berks, a large eastern county that has near 5,000 taxable inhabitants, not more than 50, and so of several others, and yet no petitions were circulated or signed in these counties. The system of conduct alluded to is the forming societies in every county in the state, who have committees of correspondence. These are now engaged in planning a uniform exertion to emancipate this state from the thraldom of despotism. A convention of deputies from every district will in all probability be agreed upon as the most eligible mode of combining the strength of the opposition, which is increasing daily both in numbers and spirit.

The Centinel, supported by the dignity of the cause he advocates, and sensible that his well-meant endeavors have met the approbation of the community, views with ineffable contempt the impotent efforts of disappointed ambition to depreciate his merit and stigmatize his performances, and without pretending to the spirit of divination, he thinks he may predict that the period is not far distant when the authors and *wilful* abettors of the new constitution will be viewed with detestation by every good man, whilst the Centinels of the present day will be honored with the esteem and confidence of a grateful people.

Great pains have been taken to discover the author of these papers, with a view, no doubt, to vilify his private character, and thereby lessen the usefulness of his writings, and many suppose they have made the discovery, but in this they are mistaken. The Centinel submits his performances to the public judgment, and challenges fair argumentation; the information he has given from time to time, has stood the test of the severest scrutiny, and thus his reputation as a writer, is established beyond the injury of his enemies. If it were in the least material to the argument or answered any one good purpose, he would not hesitate a moment in using his own signature; as it would not, but on the contrary, point where the shafts of malice could be levelled with most effect, and thus divert the public attention from the proper object, to a personal altercation, he from the first determined that the prying eye of party or curiosity should never be gratified with his real name, and to that end to be the sole depository of the secret. He has been thus explicit to prevent the repetition of the weakness of declaring off, when charged with being the author, and to put the matter upon its true footing; however, it may flatter his vanity, that these papers should be ascribed to an illustrious patriot, whose public spirit and undaunted firmness of mind, eclipse the most shining ornaments of the Roman commonwealth, in its greatest purity and glory whose persevering exertions for the public welfare, have endeared him to his country, whilst it has made every knave and aspiring despot, his inveterate enemy, and who has never condescended to deny any writings that have been ascribed to him, or to notice the railings of party.[5]

CENTINEL.

Philadelphia, April 5th, 1788.

CENTINEL NO. 19

To the PEOPLE OF PENNSYLVANIA. *Friends, Countrymen and Fellow Citizens.*

When I last addressed you on the subject of the new constitution, I had not a doubt of its rejection. The baneful nature and tendency of this system of ambition had been so fully exposed that its most zealous advocates were constrained to acknowledge many imperfections and dangers, and seemingly to acquiesce in the necessity of amendments. However, by the time this general conviction had taken place in the minds of the people, so many states had adopted the constitution and the public anxiety was so great to have an efficient government that the votaries of power and ambition were enabled by adapting their language and conduct to the temper of the times, to prevail upon a competent number of the states to establish the constitution without previous alteration upon the implied condition of subsequent amendments, which they assured would certainly be made, as every body was agreed in their propriety.

My knowledge of the principles and conduct of these men for many years past left me no room to doubt of their insincerity on this occasion. I was persuaded that all their professions of moderation and assurance of future amendments, were founded in deception, that they were but the blind of the moment, the covered way to dominion and empire. Like a barrel thrown to the whale, the people were to be amused with fancied amendments until the harpoon of power should secure its prey and render resistance ineffectual. Already the masque of ambition begins to be removed and its latent features to appear in their genuine hue, disdaining any further veil from policy; the *well-born*, inebriated with success, and despising the people for their easy credulity, think it unnecessary to dissemble any longer; almost every newspaper ridicules the idea of amendments and triumphs over the deluded people. Ye patriots of America, arouse from the dangerous infatuation in which ye are lulled, and while it is yet time, strain every nerve to rescue your country from the servile yoke of bondage and to preserve that liberty which has been so recently vindicated at the expense of so much blood and treasure. Upon the improvement of the present moment depends the fate of your country; you have now a constitutional opportunity afforded you to obtain a safe and a good government by making choice of such persons to represent you in the new congress, as have congenial sentiments with yourselves. Suffer not, ye freemen of America, the *well-born*, or their *servile minions*, to usurp the sacred trust—to impose themselves upon you as your guardians; for whatever professions they may make, or assurances they may give you, depend upon it they will deceive you: like the wolf in sheep's clothing, they will make you their prey. Treat with contempt the slanderous arts of the well-born to prejudice you against your true friends, and convince them on this great occasion, by your good sense, union and vigor, that you are not to be duped out of your liberties by all the refinements of *Machiavellian* policy. The future government of these United States will take its tone from the complexion of the first congress; upon this will greatly depend whether despotic sway, or the salutary influence of a well-regulated government shall hereafter rule this once happy land. As the legislature of this state have appointed the last Wednesday in November next for the election of the eight representatives from this state in the new congress, you ought to be prepared for that *all-important* day; and as success is only to be ensured by unanimity among the friends of equal liberty, local and personal predilections and dislikes should give place to the general sentiment. Whatever ticket may be agreed to be the majority of the opposition to the new constitution in its present shape ought to be supported by all those who are sincere in wishing for amendments. I trust that all prejudices and antipathies arising from the late war, or from difference of religion, will be sacrificed to the great object of the public welfare, and that all good and well-meaning men of whatever description will harmonize on this occasion. For among the various practices and stratagems of the well-born, the principal one, and upon which they will the most rely for success, will be the endeavor to divide you, and thus by scattering your suffrages between various candidates, to frustrate your object.

From the mode of appointment, the senate of the general government will be chiefly composed of the *well-born*, or their minions, and when we consider the great and various powers which they will possess, and their permanency, it ought to operate as an additional stimulus with you to obtain faithful representatives in the other branch of legislature, to shield your privileges and property from the machinations of ambition and the rapacity of power. The Senate, besides their proper share in the Legislature, have great executive and judicial powers—their concurrence is made necessary to all the principal appointments in government. What a fruitful source of corruption does not this present! in the capacity of Legislators they will have the irresistible temptation to institute lucrative and needless offices, as they will in fact, have the appointment of the *officers*.

When I consider the nature of power and ambition, when I view the numerous swarm of hungry office-hunters, and their splendid expectations, anticipation exhibits such a scene of rapacity and oppression, such burthensome establishments to pamper the pride and luxury of a useless herd of officers, such dissipation and profusion of the public treasure, such consequent impoverishment and misery of the people that I tremble for my country.

Such evils are only to be averted by a vigorous exertion of the freemen of America, to procure a virtuous, disinterested, and patriotic House of Representatives. That you may all view the importance of this election in its true light, and improve the only means which the constitution affords you for your preservation, is the fervent wish of

CENTINEL.

Philadelphia, October 3d, 1788.

CENTINEL NO. 20

To the CITIZENS OF PHILADELPHIA.

I congratulate my fellow citizens on the dawn of returning independence of sentiment evinced at the last election; may its ennobling influence stimulate to further and more effectual exertions; may the dictates of the *well-born junto* be treated on every occasion, with the contempt they experienced in regard to the late choice of councillor for this city.

Blinded by prejudice industriously fomented, influenced by sordid motives of private interest, or intimidated by apprehensions of being ruined in their professions, a great majority of the citizens of Philadelphia have suffered themselves to be made the scaffold upon which the *well-born junto* have ascended to the government of this state, and thereby to a predominancy in that of the United States. For several years past the essential privilege of freemen, that of electing their legislators has been reduced to unsubstantial form, to a mere farce, the appointment being really made by the junto, previous to the legal election. The situation of this city has been similar to that of Rome, under the *emperors*, who artfully gratified the people with the forms of that liberty which they had enjoyed under the republic; continuing their ostensible representatives and officers, although in fact they were the creatures of the emperors and entirely subservient to them. Thus you have been amused with the show of annual elections, and the *name* of representatives without the reality.

It may be useful to take a retrospect of the means by which this *well-born junto*, who ten years ago could not muster more than eighty-two devoted adherents in the state of Pennsylvania, have now become so formidable as to threaten the liberties of all America.

The first consideration that this review presents is, the policy by which the junto have attached to their party the weighty interest of the Quakers and Tories. In the late arduous contest with Great Britain, wherein the lives and fortunes of the Whigs were dependent upon the uncertain issue of the war, and in the course of which so much barbarity and devastation were committed by the British; it is not to be wondered at that those persons who were disaffected to the common cause, who refused to share the dangers or contribute to the expenses of the war, and on the contrary were justly suspected to be aiding and assisting a cruel and vindictive foe, should in consequence thereof, incur the resentment of the Whigs and be treated rather as enemies to their country than as fellow citizens. Hence the *test-law*, which was made to draw the line of discrimination, and to exclude from our councils those who were inimical to our cause, hence too the violence and severity with which the disaffected were treated; which has laid the foundation of the most implacable resentments and lasting prejudices.

The *junto*, considering that persons so situated and under the influence of such feelings, would make zealous adherents if they could be flattered with hopes of protection from what they deemed oppression and persecution, and still more so if they could be flattered with the pleasing prospect of a repeal of the test-law, and thereby having it in their power to assert their rights and vindicate their sufferings; the *junto* accordingly made the most liberal offers of their services to the disaffected, and as their dislike and dread of the Whigs was the cement of union, the basis upon which the *well-born* meant to build their meditated schemes of profit and aggrandizement, *Galen*,[1] and such minions were employed to aggravate the feelings and confirm the resentments of the disaffected by such misrepresentations of the principles and designs of the Whigs as to keep the former under continual apprehension of violence and rapine;[2] this persuasion had the desired effect, it riveted the disaffected so closely to the interests of the *junto* that they zealously and implicitly supported all their measures without attending to their nature or consequences. At length the liberal Whigs seeing the imposition that was practicing on the disaffected, that they were made the dupes of a set of interested designing men, resolved to convince them that their apprehensions were groundless by repealing the test-law, which excluded so many of them from the right of suffrage, and thereby putting them in a situation to judge and act for themselves; the junto who had gained so much by the subordinate situation of the disaffected were alarmed at the proposition and accordingly opposed it, which so incensed their allies that, at an election which took place soon after for a censer in the room of Col. Miles, resigned, not one of them could be persuaded to vote, and of course the constitutionalists carried the election; however the junto retrieved this *faux pas* afterwards, by the zeal they showed in procuring the repeal of the test-law.

I was always against the policy of continuing the test-law one hour longer than was absolutely necessary for the preservation of the country from a threatening enemy, as the history of other nations had taught me the injurious consequences of depriving a large proportion of the community of the important privileges of citizenship. I was aware that ambition always availed itself of such distinctions among the people to accomplish their common ruin; that the grievous oppression and misery which the Irish nation have experienced for some centuries past, have arisen from the unequal situation of the people in respect to the government—from the depressed subordinate state in which the Roman Catholics have been held, who, not having a common interest in and attachment to the government, but on the contrary highly embittered by the odious light in which they were regarded, and the severity with which they were treated, occasioned continual apprehensions to the Protestants for their safety. And this alienated state of the people, and their reciprocal enmities and suspicions, put it in the power of the English ministry, by playing one party off against the other, to keep the whole under the most submissive subjection.[3] However, the situation of the Irish nation is much improved since the liberality and harmony of sentiment that the late war gave birth to: their common danger from foreign invasion evinced the folly of their prejudices, and the necessity of union. The Irish now act in a great measure as one people, and in consequence thereof their affairs have assumed a different aspect. England has been obliged to relinquish many of the injurious monopolies and partial restrictions on the Irish commerce, and oppressive arrangements in their government. Tyranny has fled before the united voice of that people who were so lately enslaved by their internal divisions.

Another great engine of influence has been the *Bank*, which having the power of controlling the credit of every person concerned in trade, of course governed the mercantile interest, and made it entirely subservient to the views of *the well-born junto*.

It has been, moreover, the policy of the junto from the beginning to ruin, by every device of calumny and exertion of influence, the character and circumstances of every leading patriot—well knowing that the people are only important and powerful when united under confidential leaders; and as this policy was supported by a numerous and weighty party, and pursued with unremitted perseverance, the ablest and most influential patrons of the people fell victims to it. Character after character was successively attacked and hunted down by the dogs of party, with the most unfeeling rancor; even the death of the victim did not assuage their gall. In this barbarous game of policy, *Galen* bore away the palm, and shone conspicuous beyond all the imps of the *well-born*. He boasted that the superior malignity of his pen had deprived the illustrious and patriotic Reed[4] of his existence, and in his fate had made a signal example to deter others from emulating his virtues, and standing forth the advocates of the privileges of the people, which is so highly criminal in the eyes of the *well-born*.

By such means have the *well-born* attained to their present power and importance, to a situation which has enabled them to dictate and procure the establishment of a form of government for the United States, which, if not amended, will put the finishing stroke to popular liberty and confirm the sway of the *well-born*. Whilst the fate of the new constitution was doubtful, great was the assumed moderation, specious were the promises of its advocates. The despotic principles and tendency of this system of government were so powerfully demonstrated as to strike conviction in almost every breast, but this was artfully obviated by urging the pressing necessity of having an energetic government and assurance of subsequent amendments. The people were moreover told, "you will have the means in your own power to prevent the oppression of government, viz: the choice of your representatives to the federal legislature, who will be the guardians of your rights and property, your shield against the machinations of the *well-born*."

But how changed the language, how different the conduct of these men since its establishment!—they are taking effectual measures as far as in their power to realize the worst predictions of the opponents to the new constitution.—Having secured the avenue to offices under the new congress by the appointment of the senators, they are now exerting all their influence to carry the election of the representatives in the federal legislature, and thereby get the absolute command of the *purse-strings* to confirm their domination; every artifice is practicing to delude the people on this great occasion, which in all probability will be the last opportunity they will have to preserve their liberties, as the new congress will have it in their power to establish despotism without violating the principles of the constitution. The proposed meeting at Lancaster is a high game of deception; under the appearance of giving the people an opportunity to nominate their representatives, the minions of ambition are to be palmed upon them. Ostensible deputies are to be sent from every county for this purpose, who, if we may judge from those already appointed, will take especial care to prevent the nomination of men who have congenial feelings with the people, as such would prove troublesome obstacles in the way of ambition; the intention is to monopolize both branches of the legislature and make the government harmonize with the aggrandizement of the *well-born* and their minions.

The deputies appointed to go from this city characterize the juggle and designate the intention more strikingly than is in the power of language to express or the ingenuity of artifice to conceal; the man who confessedly has had a principal share in the framing of a constitution that is universally allowed to be dangerously despotic, and therefore to require great amendments; the man who in every stage of its adoption has been its greatest advocate; whose views of aggrandizement are founded upon the unqualified execution of this government, whose aristocratic principles, aspiring ambition, and contempt of the common people have long distinguished him; I say this man is now selected as one of that body who are to dictate the choice of the people—to point out *faithful* representatives who are to check ambition and defend their rights and privileges. If the people suffer themselves to be thus fooled upon so momentous an occasion, they will deserve their fate. But I am persuaded they will discern the fraud and act becoming freemen, that they will give their suffrages to real patriots and genuine representatives.

CENTINEL.

Philadelphia, October 22nd, 1788.

111

To the PEOPLE OF PENNSYLVANIA. *Friends and Countrymen.*
France exhibits at this moment one of the most interesting scenes
to human nature, and peculiarly instructive to the citizens of the United
States,[1]—a people who for many centuries had been accustomed to
yield implicit obedience to the mandates of royalty, who never presumed to judge of the propriety of any measure of government, but
whose highest glory was to recommend itself to the idol on the throne
by the most obsequious services, to sacrifice every manly feeling,
every consideration whether of self or country, at the shrine of his
grandeur; I say this people, so long obsequious and subservient to
the will and pleasure of a despot, seem to have imbibed a new nature,
to be animated with the noblest, most enlightened sentiments of patriotism, and in opposition to a court supported by a standing army of
200,000 mercenaries, is asserting its rights and privileges. Various
causes have concurred to produce this astonishing revolution of sentiments and conduct in the people of France: perhaps the divine writings of a Montesquieu laid the foundation, and doubtless the able,
animated discussion of the native rights of mankind occasioned by
the late contest between America and Britain, must have been very
instrumental in effecting this general illumination and inspiring this
ardent love of liberty in France. But it is probable from the strength
which arbitrary power had acquired by custom and long-established
habits of obedience, that it might have continued in uninterrupted
exercise for a long time to come, if the French court had not precipitated its destruction by an extraordinary stretch of power, which struck
at all the remaining privileges of the people, and aimed at the unqualified establishment of despotism.

The French, enlightened to their native rights had availed themselves of institutions and provincial privileges, hitherto enjoyed but
in name, to check the despotism of power, which, insensible of the
great change of sentiment that had taken place in France, was so rash
as to attempt the enforcement of new arrangements and impositions,
instead of adhering to the old establishments that time and custom
had sanctioned. The French nation, already prepared, wanted but a
suitable occasion to vindicate their rights: this was now afforded by
the indiscretion of the court, and they embraced it by reviving the
exercise of the long-dormant privilege of their parliaments to nega-

112

tive the arrets of the court, by refusing to register such of them as they disapproved, without which they could not be legally executed.

The French court, finding their projects of power and dominion frustrated by the patriotism of these local parliaments, who, from their vicinity and near connection with the people, were greatly influenced by the common feelings and interest, came to the bold resolution of annihilating them at one stroke, and substituting in lieu of them one general parliament, or *court pleniere*, under the specious pretence of reinstating the public finances and credit, deranged and prostrated by the late expensive war and the peculations of the ministers of state.

But the French nation had too much discernment to be thus imposed on: they saw the object and tendency of the new constitution, or *court pleniere*; they were sensible that a parliament so remote from the people would be wholly subservient to the views of the court, however despotic they might be; they had experienced the fidelity, the patriotism, and the fellow-feeling of their provincial parliaments too much to acquiesce in their annihilation; and accordingly they opposed this decisive step of the court with a spirit, and suspended, if not frustrated, the intended innovation.

What a surprising familiarity there is in this project of the French court and that of our *would-be despots!* The Cæsars of this country, having been baffled in all their attempts upon the liberties of the separate states, by the patriotism and vigilance of the representatives of the people in the state legislatures, they have availed themselves a peculiar crisis of trade and public affairs, of the universal wish to vest congress with competent powers, to procure the establishment of a general government, or *court pleniere*, that will from its constitution grasp all powers and silently abrogate the state governments.

In the conduct and example of the French provincial parliaments we have a striking illustration of the great utility and indeed necessity of local or provincial governments being vested with competent power to prevent the oppression of the general government, who being so far removed from the people, would possess neither the means or the disposition to consult and promote their interests and felicity. The provincial parliaments of France, although infinitely inferior in their constitution and independency to our state legislatures, have proved an efficient obstacle to the extension of arbitrary power, and in all probability will be the instruments of procuring a constitution of government that will secure the enjoyment of the inestimable blessings of liberty to every citizen of France.

Our *grandees*, apprehensive that the opposition making by the French nation to the abolition of their provincial parliaments, and against the establishment of the new constitution, or *court pleniere*, might from similarity of principles and circumstances, open the eyes of the Americans to the despotism aimed at in our new constitution or *court pleniere*, has endeavored to conceal the true nature of the convulsions by which France is at present agitated; and in this view, in contradiction to the most authentic information both public and private, they have industriously circulated the idea that the designs of the French court are patriotic and in favor of the people, and that the opposition to their measures proceeds from a set of interested men, who wish to exempt themselves from the common burthens; but where is the American patriot who credits this representation, when he sees a *Fayette*, an *Armand*, among the foremost in this opposition, when he beholds the magnanimity and heroism displayed by this opposition who, fearless of the frowns and persecution of the court, persevere in the defense of their rights, esteeming banishment, imprisonment, loss of offices and emoluments, highly honorable when incurred in such a cause?

Galen, who in common with those of his party, had experienced the galling mortification of being defeated in every attempt to overthrow our invaluable state constitution, declared in the Convention, "that he rejoiced at the prospect which the establishment of the new constitution afforded of the state governments being laid at the feet of Congress." This sentiment, which the Doctor had indiscreetly suffered to escape from him in the hour of insolence and triumph, was afterwards ingeniously explained away, lest the people should be apprised of the real object in view by this premature discovery; for James the Caledonian, the principal framer and advocate of the new constitution, had been obliged to confess, that so extensive a country as the United States include, could not be governed on the principles of freedom by one consolidated government, but that such a one must necessarily be supremely despotic.

114

My next number will be on the subject of the immense sums of public money unaccounted for, now ascertained by a late investigation of Congress, which perhaps will be the most effectual method of elucidating the principles of a number of the great advocates of the new constitution, and enable the public to form a better judgment of one of the men lately appointed by the legislature of this State to a seat in the Federal senate and of some of the men proposed as Federal representatives, who will be found to be but puppets to this great public defaulter.

CENTINEL.

Philadelphia, November 6, 1788.

CENTINEL NO. 22

To the PEOPLE OF PENNSYLVANIA. *Friends and Fellow Citizens.*

It was my intention to appropriate this number to the consideration of the enormous sums of public money unaccounted for by individuals, now ascertained by a late investigation of Congress; but accidentally meeting with an address to the freemen of Pennsylvania, signed *Lucullus,* published in the *Federal Gazette* of November 6th, I thought no time should be lost in detecting the atrocious falsehoods, and counteracting the baneful poison contained in that address. In a former number I noticed the base policy practised by the *Republicans*, as they styled themselves, of imitating and prejudicing that part of the community who were disaffected to our cause in the late war against the constitutional Whigs, by the grossest calumny and misrepresentation of their conduct and principles, and thereby duping the disaffected into the support of measures, which their dispassionate judgment would have reprobated as highly injurious to the common welfare. That address is a continuation of the same policy, and from characteristic features, is known to be the production of Galen, who has done more to destroy the harmony of Pennsylvania, and forward the vassalage of her citizens to the *rich and aspiring* than all the other firebrands of party and instruments of ambition.[1]

We are now hastening to a crisis that will determine the fate of this great country—that will decide whether the United States is to be ruled by a free government, or subjected to the supremacy of a *lordly and profligate few*. Hitherto the gratification of party spirit and prejudice was attended with the ruin of the honest Whigs and the emolument and aggrandizement of the *Republicans* at the common expense; but now it would be attended with the loss of all liberty and the establishment of a general thraldom—men of all descriptions, except our rulers, would equally wear the fetters, and experience the evils of despotism; it therefore behooves every man who has any regard for the welfare and happiness of his country, of himself, or his posterity, to endeavor to divest himself of all prejudices that may bias or blind his judgment on this great occasion. In confidence of a dispassionate perusal and consideration, I will now take up the address and expose its fallacy. It begins, "You will be called upon on the last Wednesday of the present month to give your votes for *eight* persons to represent you in the Legislature of the United States. You never were called upon to exercise the privilege of electing rulers upon a more important occasion. Two tickets will be offered you. The one will contain men who will support the new constitution *in its present form*: the other ticket will contain men who will overset the government under the specious pretext of amending it." Here is a plain, explicit avowal that the new constitution is to be supported in its *present form*; I hope this declaration will open the eyes of those people who have been deluded by the deceitful promises of amendments, and that being thereby convinced of the fallacy of the reiterated assurances of amendments, they will now embrace the only method left of obtaining them, by giving their suffrages and influence to the other ticket. The bugbear raised to intimidate the people from voting for this ticket, viz: "that the design is to destroy the government under the specious pretext of amending it," I trust will be treated with the deserved contempt, and that this low device will only confirm the people the more in their determination to support men favorable to amendments. The address proceeds, "To give you just ideas of the anti-federal ticket, I shall only add that it was composed and will be supported by persons who violated the rights of conscience by imposing a wicked and tyrannical *test-law* upon the Quakers, Mennonists, and other sects of Christians who hold war to be unlawful." In regard to the *test-law*, I shall only observe that the circumstances of the times justified, nay, made it indispensably necessary; that it was a dictate of common sense and agreeable to the great law of self-preservation to draw a line of discrimination, and exclude from our councils and places of power and trust those persons who were inimical to our cause; and that such has been, and must ever be, from the nature of things, the practice of all nations when engaged in civil war. However, I am clearly of opinion that sound policy dictates the repeal of such laws as soon as it can be done consistent with the public safety, to prevent men of such principles and views as *Galen* and his party from availing themselves of the irritated feelings of the non-jurors and their friends, to compass designs prejudicial to the public liberties and welfare.

The *tender law* stands next in the catalogue of crimes. "Who ruined half the widows, orphans and aged citizens in the State, by an unjust and cruel tender law?" In order to form a judgment of the propriety of this law, we must recur to the occasion of making it. When the thirteen late provinces, now States of America, in Congress assembled, came to the resolution of supporting their liberty and independence by the sword, they found it necessary to anticipate the resources of the country by emitting bills of credit; and as the value and efficiency of this means depended on their being received in all transactions equal to gold and silver money of like denominations, a legal compulsion to ensure this currency to them was *then* deemed essentially necessary, and accordingly Congress recommended the measure to the several States, who, in compliance therewith, passed laws making the continental money a legal tender. This paper money was the sinew of the war, and as such was to be cherished—upon its credit depended our political salvation. However, it is my decided opinion that Congress was mistaken in supposing that the credit of paper money could be supported by making it a legal tender: it is adequate funds of redemption being provided, and public confidence only that can stamp the value of money on paper.

But why censure the Government of Pennsylvania for laws that were made ministerially, in compliance with the recommendation of Congress? May not every government in the union be stigmatized on the same principle, as they all passed similar laws? Moreover, with what consistency can the *Republicans* adduce the tender laws as a crime against the *Constitutionalists*, when the former were the authors of the most oppressive of them, when they renewed these laws after they had been suspended by the Constitutionalists? A recurrents to the minutes of the assembly and the laws of the State will fully establish this fact. It will thereby appear that the assembly elected in October 1779, who were to a man Constitutionalists, suspended the operation of the laws making the continental money a legal tender for three months, by their act passed on the 31st May, 1780, which was further continued by their act of the 22d of September following; and by the succeeding assembly, which were *Republicans*, it was continued without limitation. Thus the legal tender of the continental money was first suspended by the Constitutionalists; and this same assembly passed a law, on the 25th March, 1780, for emitting £100,000 in bills of credit, founded on the City Lots and Province Island, without making them a legal tender.

It will also appear by the minutes of Assembly and laws, that the Republicans afterwards, viz., on the 9th of April, 1781, emitted the enormous sum of £500,000 in bills of credit, at a time when the public exigencies did not require or justify this oppressive emission of paper money, and could only be accounted for by the scene of profitable speculation that was made on this money by the *Cofferer*[2] and his friends; and this paper the Republicans made a legal tender, with heavy forfeitures and penalties in case of refusal.

The Republicans moreover made the £100,000 island money emitted by the Constitutionalists a legal tender, although the fund of redemption was so abundantly adequate, the consequence of which was a greater depreciation. And these tender laws were not made in pursuance of recommendations of Congress, but were the original acts of the Republicans.

If the *tender laws* have been so cruel and wicked, so destructive as "to ruin half the widows, orphans, and aged citizens in the state," how came the immaculate Republicans to renew them at so late a period in the war, when they must have been fully informed of their operation, and when they had not so good a plea to justify them? What unparalleled impudence to charge the *Constitutionalists* with the hardships and evils of laws that they, the Republicans, were instrumental in reviving and continuing! And yet as extravagant and inconsistent as this charge is, the prejudice and credulity of party spirit has implicitly believed it. Although the Republican party devised and made the last *tender laws* for their private emolument, although *they* reaped the rich harvest of speculations on the public credit by means of these laws, yet the Constitutionalists must bear all the odium of *them*.

The *Doctor* has exhibited a most exaggerated picture of the grievous consequences of the *militia law*; he says "that wagons have been sold for 3s. 9d, cows for 9d, etc." Whoever reprobates the militia law, must on the same principle reprobate the late glorious contest for liberty; for any person the least acquainted with the transactions of the war, must know that the militia were very instrumental to our success; a law was therefore necessary to form and call forth this militia when requisite. If, in the execution of a general system, hardships have happened to individuals, they are to be considered as private misfortunes, not public oppressions; or if collectors and other officers have prostituted this law to private gain, they are to be stigmatized, not the law or its framers.

The address continues, "who have pocketed, or squandered away as much confiscated property as would have paid, if it had been properly disposed of, half the debt of the state!" This is a charge easily made, but until the mere assertion of an anonymous writer is deemed sufficient to substantiate the fact, the public will expect better evidence. I call upon the doctor to name the instances, point out the persons, and produce the proof of this peculation on the confiscated property; and in answer to the other part of the charge, viz: "that it was squandered," I will say it is equally groundless, whether as to the appropriation that was made of this property, or as to the premature disposition of it; for if we may judge from the temper and conduct of succeeding houses of assembly, it is evident that had the sales of this property been postponed, they would never have taken place, as it would have been restored to the original owners.

The address proceeds, "who have banished specie and credit from the state, by their last emission of paper money. Who have nearly ruined the state by assuming and funding the debts of the United States, whereby they have checked our agriculture, commerce and manufactures, and driven many thousands of farmers and mechanics to Kentucky and Niagara." If an honest, just compliance with public engagements, if the support of public credit, so prized by every wise nation and inviolably maintained by the enlightened government of *Great Britain*, as its great resource in time of need, is considered criminal in *Pennsylvania*, the funding law and the last emission of paper money cannot be vindicated; but I am persuaded the people of this state have too high a sense of justice and too much discernment to their permanent interests for this doctrine to become popular.

"Who have burdened the state with expensive establishments and salaries, thereby encouraging idleness, dependence and servility among our citizens." This is a groundless assertion and base calumny.

"Who have violated the constitution of the state by sacrilegiously robbing an institution of learning and charity of its charter funds." I refer my readers to the reasons of the majority of the council of censors, for a complete refutation of this charge.

"Who by the number and weight of their taxes, have reduced landed property to one fourth of its former value, and thereby forced many ancient and respectable farmers and merchants, possessed of large visible estates, to submit to the operations of laws which have reduced them from well-earned affluence or independence to poverty and misery." How lost to all sense of truth and decency must the Doctor be to ascribe the evils of the oppressive taxes to the *Constitutionalists*, when he knows his party were the authors of them? Does he forget the enormous tax of 1782, imposed by his friend Mr. *Morris*, which vastly exceeded the ability of the people to pay, amounting to £425,000 in specie besides the paper money?—a tax that has been productive of more distress and mischief than the aggregate of all the previous and subsequent taxes, and is the efficient cause of our present difficulties in taxation; and does the Doctor forget the other numerous taxes imposed by the same party, some of them to favor their speculations in the paper moneys?

"Who have opposed the adoption of the Federal government by the grossest falsehoods, by the abuse of the best characters in the United States, and by an attempt to excite a civil war." A review of the discussion of the new constitution will expose the fallacy of this charge; whilst sound reason and well-supported arguments were made use of by the opposition, scurrility and abuse of every person who dared to object to the new constitution, were lavished by the Federalists, and if there was any danger of a civil war, it arose from their violence and precipitance in forcing down the government without giving the people time or opportunity to examine or judge for themselves.

"Who aim at nothing but power or office—who have nothing to lose, and everything to hope, from a general convulsion." This comes very consistently from a party which abounds in needy office hunters, whose staunch federalisms and obsequious services are founded on, and stimulated by, the ravishing prospect of sharing in the great loaves and fishes of the United States, under the new constitution.

"Whose private characters are as profligate as their public conduct has been oppressive, dishonest, and selfish, and who, instead of aiming to share in the honors of the new government, should retire in silent gratitude for having escaped those punishments to which their numerous frauds, oppressions and other crimes, have justly exposed them." If I was disposed to recriminate—there is an ample field—I would begin with the *cofferer*, the head of the other party, and trace his character through the numerous speculations on the public, from his appointment to the c—l a—y of the United States, to his resignation as f—r; I would delineate the corrupt principles and conduct of the rest of the party down to the herd of base parasites and minions, the Doctor included, who would make a conspicuous figure in the black picture. On the other hand, I challenge the Doctor or his associates to sully the integrity, the disinterested conduct of the leaders of the constitutional party, by any colorable charge of peculation or abuse of the public trusts so often confided to them. Like the virtuous *Fabricius*, they retired from offices of the highest eminence and opportunities of embezzling the public treasure, with unpolluted hands and native integrity; so far from growing rich in the public service, they have impaired their own fortunes by their zeal and contributions for the public welfare; and instead of receiving applause for their patriotism, they are loaded with obloquy, are vilified and stigmatized with that poverty.[3] How ungenerous and inconsistent! At the same time I must confess, that there have been villains of the constitutional party, for perfection is not to be expected on this side eternity. But it has been the good fortune of this party, that the instances have been rare and of an inferior kind; they did not ascend to the principals of the party, to the great influential leading characters, who gave the complexion and tone to the measures of government.

The foregoing remarks upon the first part of the address apply equally to the remainder, and prove the fallacy and turpitude of the whole of it.

CENTINEL.

Philadelphia, November 12th, 1788.

CENTINEL NO. 23

To the PEOPLE OF PENNSYLVANIA. *Friends and Fellow Citizens.*

I have promised a number on the subject of the enormous sums of public moneys unaccounted for by individuals, now ascertained by a late investigation of Congress, but find so extensive a field opened, as to require many numbers to treat of the several parts in a proper manner; I shall, therefore, confine my remarks at present to one paragraph of it. This investigation, after being long suppressed, has at length reached the public eye, and is of such magnitude and exhibits such immense peculations on the public treasure by men who now assume the lead in this and some other of the state governments, and are among the most distinguished patrons of the new constitution, as to demand the serious attention of the citizens of the United States at this peculiar crisis of public affairs.

Unawed by that power and influence, that false glare of reputation and by that clamor and partiality of party spirit, which for many years had rendered the characters of the great public defaulters sacred and impervious to public scrutiny, the Centinel, regardless of consequences in such a cause, impeached them at the bar of the public; he charged them with the receipt of millions of public money, for which they had not accounted; and notwithstanding he produced sufficient documents to substantiate the charge—such was the shameless effrontery of these men and their minions on the one hand, and the confirmed prejudice and partiality of the public on the other hand, that the Centinel was deemed a *libeller*, a *calumniator* of some of the best and most illustrious characters in the United States. So immaculate was the *Cofferer* considered, that the epithets of rascal, villain etc., were lavished upon every person who dared to assert anything to his prejudice, and the cry of a cruel persecution was raised against the Centinel and others for endeavoring to compel him to disgorge the public treasure.

Congress have now confirmed the charges adduced by the Centinel against Mr. *Robert Morris* and the other great public defaulters, so that if any person hereafter advocates the principles and measures of these men, he will thereby acknowledge congenial sentiments and proclaim his own character—the public will be equally aware of the one as of the other.

In my seventeenth number, there is the following paragraph: "When we consider the immense sums of public money taken up by

123

Mr. Morris, as commercial agent, to import military supplies, and even to trade on behalf of the United States, at a time when the risk was so great that individuals would not venture their property; that all these transactions were conducted under the private firm of *Willing* and *Morris*, which afforded unrestrained scope to peculation and embezzlement of the public property, by enabling Mr. Morris to throw the loss of all captures by the enemy at that hazardous period on the public, and converting most of the safe arrivals (which were consequently very valuable) into his private property; and when we add to these considerations, the principles of the *man*, his bankrupt situation at the commencement of the war, and the immense wealth he has dazzled the world with since, can it be thought unreasonable to conclude that the principal source of his wealth was the commercial agency of the United States during the war?—not that I would derogate from his successful ingenuity in his numerous speculations in the paper moneys, Havannah monopoly and job, or in the sphere of financiering."

And in a piece which I wrote under the signature of *"One of the People,"* published in the *Independent Gazetteer* of April 17th last, I referred to a report of a committee of Congress of the 11th of February, 1779, to prove that Mr. Morris was a member of the secret or commercial committee, and that this committee had authorized and entrusted him *solely* with the purchasing of produce in the different states, and exporting the same on the public account, and that all such contracts were made by him under the private firm of *Willing* and *Morris*.

Mr. Morris being absent in Virginia when the Centinel made the foregoing charge against him, his friends and minions undertook the vindication of his character; they asserted that he had rendered his accounts as commercial agent, and that they were settled; but Mr. Morris, sensible that the ground which his advocates had taken for his justification was not tenable, and that their officious zeal had led them to make assertions that could easily be disproved, was obliged to confess that he had not settled, or even rendered his accounts as commercial agent, at the distant period of ten years after his transactions in that capacity; but with his usual ingenuity endeavored to apologize for not doing it, as will appear by a recurrence to his address to the public, dated Richmond, March 21st, and published in the *Independent Gazetteer* of April 8th last.

I will make an extract of this address containing Mr. Morris's acknowledgment of receiving the public money and his not settling his accounts. It is as follows, viz.: "At an early period of the revolution, I contracted with the committees to import arms, ammunition and clothing, and was employed to export American produce, and make remittances on account of the United States, for the purpose of lodging funds in Europe. To effect these objects, I received considerable sums of money. The business has been performed, but the accounts are not yet settled".

Having stated the charge formerly made against Mr. Morris and the evidences that was then in power to establish it, I will now add a quotation from the late investigation made by Congress, extracted from their journals of the 30th September last, viz.: "Your committee turning their attention to an act of Congress on the 22d of May last, directing the board of treasury to call upon all such persons as had been entrusted with public money, and had neglected to account for the same, and such other persons as had made partial or vague settlements, without producing proper vouchers, were desirous to obtain a particular statement of the accounts which are in the above predicament; but they are sorry to find that such a detail is too lengthy to be here inserted. Some of those accounts are stated in the file of papers marked *papers respecting unsettled accounts*, which is herewith submitted. From the general aspect of those accounts, your committee are constrained to observe, that there are many former transactions respecting the public treasures. No less a sum than 2,122,600 dollars has been advanced to the secret committee of Congress, before August 2d, 1777, and a considerable part of this money remains to be accounted for otherwise than by contracts made with individuals of their own body, while those individuals neglect to account."

Thus it appears that a considerable part of the enormous sum of two millions, one hundred twenty-two thousand and six hundred dollars, nearly equal to specie, which was advanced to the secret committee of Congress, remains unaccounted for, otherwise than by contracts made with individuals of their *own* body, *while those individuals neglected to account*. And who those individuals are is evident from the report of the committee of Congress on the 11th of February, 1779, before quoted, and from other records of Congress. By them it appears, that after the death of Mr. *Ward*, who was the first chairman and agent of the *secret* committee, which happened very early, before this committee had transacted much business, that Mr. Robert Morris was solely entrusted by the secret committee with the disposition of the public money advanced to them, and that all his transactions as commercial agent, were conducted by him under the private firm of Willing and Morris.

Eleven years have now elapsed since Mr. Morris was entrusted with the disposition of near two millions of specie dollars, and no account of this immense sum has yet been rendered by him. What conclusion must every dispassionate person make of this delinquency? Is it not more than probable that he has converted the public money to his own property, and that, fearful of detection, and reluctant to refund, he has, and will, as long as he is able, avoid an investigation and settlement of these long standing accounts?

I will ask, did the majority of the late assembly evince either wisdom or virtue, when they appointed this man to a seat in the *federal senate*, or will the people evidence any regard to their own interests if they give their suffrages to his creatures, who are now proposed as federal representatives? Under the administration of such men, is it rational to expect that public defaulters will be called to account, or that future peculation and pocketing of the public money will be discouraged or detected?

I intend in future numbers to notice the other numerous instances of public defaulters, and to show that if it had not been for the immense peculations and pocketing of the public moneys by individuals, and those among our most distinguished *Federalists*, that the people would not have been burdened with above one-third of the present national debt and consequent taxes.

The following article of the last report of the committee of congress on the finances, will be the subject of my next number, viz.: "Your committee were desirous to discover in what manner the large sums of money received in France have been accounted for, but the subject of this inquiry seems to be involved in darkness.

	Livres	s.	d.
The amount of the several receipts is	47,111,859	12	S
Of this sum there has been sent over or drawn for and expended in America 26,246,727 5 5			
Salaries of foreign ministers 1,160,183			
	27,406,910	5	5
There remains	19,704,949	7	3

"The documents for the expenditures of this balance have never been produced at the treasury. They must be in France if there are any such papers. A full inquiry into the premises now claims the attention of the board of treasury. Some time must be expended in making the necessary investigation, but the result may be of important service to the United States."

In the investigation of this article, which informs us of a deficiency of upwards of nineteen millions of livres specie, however it may offend, I must expose the names of the men who have received this money.

CENTINEL.

Philadelphia, November 17, 1788.

To the PEOPLE OF PENNSYLVANIA. *Friends and Fellow Citizens.* This number was appropriated to the investigation of that article of the last report of a committee of Congress, which informs us of a deficiency of NINETEEN MILLIONS of livres SPECIE, in the moneys entrusted to our *Commissioners* in *France*, the principal of whom was the Honorable BENJAMIN FRANKLIN the sanction of whose name has given such weight and success to the new constitution; but I shall be obliged to postpone the discussion of this subject in order to notice Mr. *Morris's* answer published in the *Independent Gazetteer* of this morning to my last number.

Mr. Morris, presuming upon the strength and continuance of those prejudices which his ingenuity and address had so successfully raised, and which for many years had blinded the public to his real principles and conduct, and enabled him to prosecute his schemes of profit and aggrandizement to an immense extent, without detection or jealousy, has now the effrontery to treat the serious, well founded charges of the CENTINEL, and a report of a committee of Congress, with supercilious contempt, and to suppose that his unsupported assertions in a matter where he is so deeply interested, will be implicitly believed by that public whose property, to the amount of millions, he was entrusted with above eleven years ago, and for which he has not yet accounted.

Mr. Morris says, "On the repeated slanders of my enemies, so far as they can affect myself, I look down with silent contempt; but as I have been lately honored with a high trust in the federal government, and as an attempt is made to wound the federal cause by attacks on my reputation and the conduct of those who appointed me to a seat in the senate, *my attachment to that cause*, and my respect for my fellow citizens, lead me to inform them that I have lately been at New York for the purpose of bringing forward a settlement of my accounts with the United States, and they are now in a *train* of investigation, and that I shall do everything in my power to obtain a final settlement of them before the meeting of Congress under the new constitution."

Is it slander to call upon a public officer to account for the disposition of millions of public money entrusted to him above eleven years ago? Or is it slander to denominate such a man a public de-

128

faulter? Can any reasonable or honest obstacle have so long delayed the settlement of his accounts, especially when we consider the abilities and accuracy of this man in accounts, and his persevering diligence and assiduity to business? Is it now probable that he really means to render his accounts, when we advert to the unsuccessful exertions of a series of the greatest characters in Congress to compel him to account, and who for more than eleven years have been baffled in all their virtuous and patriotic attempts by the predominant influence and the machinations of this man and his minions? What have become of the labors of *Manheim*, where Mr. Morris retired at a gloomy and doubtful crisis of public affairs under the avowed pretence of preparing these very accounts for settlement? Where is the man besides Mr. Morris, who can thus act and preserve any character or confidence, or who with so serious and weighty a charge against him would continue to be preferred to the highest honors and trusts of his country, with the power of screening past delinquencies, and the opportunity of further speculations; or who would be supported and justified by so numerous and powerful a party?

As an instance of Mr. Morris's dangerous influence, and also of his reluctance to have his accounts, even as superintendent of finance, investigated, it may be observed that the public spirited men in Congress on the 21st of June, 1785, procured, with great difficulty, against the strenuous opposition and low subterfuges of Mr. Morris's friends and minions, a resolution of that honorable body to this effect, that three commissioners be appointed to examine the receipts and expenditures of the late superintendent of finance; but this resolution was the only consequence of this virtuous effort, for Mr. Morris has been able to prevent any Commissioners being appointed in pursuance of this resolution entered into above three years since. It is true that very lately the disinterested part of Congress, strengthened by the attacks made by the Centinel and others upon the great public defaulters, and the consequent clamor of the people, have, against the secret inclination of a majority of Congress, obtained resolutions and appointments of officers to compel the public defaulters to account and restore the public moneys; but the efficacy of these resolutions and appointments entirely depends on the complexion of the Congress under the new constitution; for if the great public defaulters and their minions be elected, it would be ridiculous to suppose that they would countenance scrutiny into the conduct of themselves and patrons. Mr. Morris, sensible that if he can carry his creatures who are proposed as representatives in the new Congress, he may laugh at and *really* contemn any future attempts to call him to account, has, therefore, at the eve of the approaching decisive election promised to settle and account for the immense sums of public money that he received above eleven years ago, and even assures that he has been at New York lately on this business and that his accounts are in a *train* of investigation But like the Manheim investigation promised as seriously eight or nine years ago, the present will prove to have no other existence than in the deception of the moment, and this *train* will be found delusive and without end.

My fellow citizens, suffer not yourselves to be thus continually imposed on by a man whose whole career in public life has been marked by delinquencies in money concerns; but make choice of such men to represent you as will secure your liberties and property. And as you are now well acquainted with the principles and views of Mr. Morris, you are enabled to form a proper opinion of Messrs. *Fitzsimons*, *Clymer*, etc., who for ten years past have been the devoted instruments and partisans of Mr. Morris, and participators in his numerous speculations. CENTINEL.

Philadelphia, Saturday Noon, November 22d, 1788.

Notes

The text of this edition of the *Letters of Centinel* is based on that found in John B. McMaster and Frederick D. Stone, *Pennsylvania and the Federal Constitution, 1787-1788* (Philadelphia, 1888). A few obvious typographical errors have been corrected. The time will no doubt come when a complete, scholarly edition of Samuel Bryan's writings, along with a critical biography of him, will be required. The purpose of this edition is extremely modest: to provide readers with a convenient edition of the letters.

Conversations with Dr. A. Bronson Feldman (1914 -1982), my teacher and friend, and with Donald LaGreca, a friend and a teacher in the public schools of Philadelphia, helped me in preparing the following notes. I have also relied heavily on the *Dictionary of American Biography*.

Centinel No. 1—Published in *The Independent Gazetteer*, October 5, 1787. (Pages 6-16)

1. The names referred to here are no doubt those of George Washington and Benjamin Franklin. Centinel later explicitly objects to the way the names of these popular and respected figures were, in his view, used to mislead the public.

2. Centinel again clearly refers to Washington and Franklin. Washington had presided over the Constitutional convention but took little part in the debates. Franklin, aging and ill, clearly sought a compromise. According to a perhaps apocryphal story, when asked "Are we to have a monarchy or a republic?" by a woman in Philadelphia after the convention adjourned, Franklin replied, "A republic—if you can keep it."

3. This early critical, not to say devastating, examination of the theory of governmental checks and balances did nothing to keep the phrase from becoming a popular political mantra.

4. Centinel's insistence on "the sense of the people at large" as "the only operative and efficient check" on governors clearly places him in the tradition of the Declaration of Independence. His resistance to change was a way of keeping faith with the principles of the American Revolution. The movement to adopt the unamended Constitution was a radical attempt to undo the American Revolution: it was a bloodless counter-revolution.

5. Centinel's conditions for a free government—a virtuous populace and property "pretty equally divided"—point to the two ways free government in the United States has been repeatedly and effectively prevented: by rendering the populace befuddled and by wallowing in an extremely uneven division of property. Anyone who accepts Centinel's position here is forced to conclude that, since the United States government is now neither an aristocracy nor a monarchy, it must be a despotism.

6. It is a quirk of history that Centinel two hundred years ago fingered what has recently become a subject of political debate— the need for "term limits."

7. There is an Orwellian aspect to the debate over the Constitution. The so-called Federalists in fact opposed a federal government and favored a national government. The so-called Anti-federalists favored a federal government and opposed a national government. The lie worked itself out by our continuing to call our national government the Federal government. One side effect of this semantic solution to the lie is for historians and others to heap abuse on the Articles of Confederation ritualistically, without a great deal of thought or examination.

Centinel No. 2—Published in the *Freeman's Journal*, October 24, 1787. (Pages 17-30)

1. John Dickinson (November 8, 1732-February 14, 1808) whose *Letters from a Farmer in Pennsylvania to the Inhabitants of the British Colonies* (1768) did much to educate the population and prepare it for revolution. He took part in the debates over the Constitution as a delegate to the Convention of 1787 from Delaware. His letters signed "Fabius" favored adoption of the Constitution.

2. James Wilson (September 14, 1742-August 21, 1798), born in Scotland, became a tutor in Latin at the College of Philadelphia in February 1766. He turned to law and prepared for the bar by working in John Dickinson's office for two years. Politically active for the rest of his life, he is best remembered as the head— or at least the figurehead—of "the conservatives" of Pennsylvania, that is, those dedicated to the overthrow of popular sover-

eignty. His speech seems to have been an immediate, public response to *Centinel No. 1*.

3. Centinel here, as elsewhere, shows in detail the inconsistency of the "conservative" or "Federalist" position, using their arguments in support of the Revolution against their support of the Constitution.

4. It must be remembered that the delegates to what is now called the Constitutional Convention were gathered to recommend amendments to the Articles of Confederation, not to draft a new plan of government. The legality of the actions of the Convention can still be debated. This half-hearted approach of Congress in forwarding the draft of the Constitution to the states underscores the document's dubious status.

5. Wilson

6. Convention

Centinel No. 3—Published in *The Independent Gazetteer*, November 8, 1787. (Pages 31-38)

1. Centinel again tries to offset the influence of the support of the Constitution by Washington and Franklin here. Franklin was one of the two delegates from Pennsylvania Centinel did not believe to be "ambitious and designing." The other was probably Jared Ingersoll.

2. The tactics of the so-called Federalists are repeatedly shown to have been the tactics of despots and more recent enemies of democracy—the Communists, the Fascists, the Mob, Arab sheiks, and our so-called Intelligence Community, to name a few.

3. The following statement is given as a note to the original:

"The message of the President and Council, sent into the present General Assembly on the 27th of October last, discloses another imposition. The Board sent to the House the official transmission of the proposed constitution of the United States, inclosed in a letter from the President of Congress, which proves that the paper produced to the last House on the day before the final rising of the same, was a surreptitious copy of the vote of Congress, obtained for the purpose of deluding the Legislature into the extravagance of directing an election of Convention within *nine* days.

"The provision made by the Convention of Pennsylvania, which sat in 1776 for amending the constitution, is guarded with admirable wisdom and caution. A Council of Censors is to be holden every seven years, which shall have power (two-thirds of the whole number elected agreeing) to propose amendments of the same government, to call a Convention to adopt and establish these propositions; but the alterations must be "promulgated *at least* six months before the day appointed for the *election* of such Convention, for the previous consideration of the people, that they may have an opportunity of instructing their delegates on the subject." The present measures explain the conduct of a certain party of the Censors, who sat in 1784 (much fewer than two-thirds of the whole), that proposed to abolish the 47th article of the constitution, whereby the manner of amending the same was regulated."

4.   "Brutus" was the pen name of Robert Yates (January 27, 1738-September 9, 1801) who had been a delegate from New York to the 1787 Convention along with John Lansing and Alexander Hamilton. Yates and Lansing left the Convention on July 5, 1787, on the ground the Convention was exceeding its powers by writing a new plan of government. Yates and Governor George Clinton were leading "anti-federalists" in New York. Clinton was, along with Jefferson, among those to whom Samuel Bryan identified himself as the author of the Centinel letters. Yates's notes on the debates and proceedings of the Convention of 1787 were published in 1821. It should be remembered that the delegates of the Convention met behind closed doors and agreed to keep the debates secret.

5.   Publishers of the *Pennsylvania Packet*, a Philadelphia newspaper. They first published the Constitution on September 19, 1787.

Centinel No. 4—Published in *The Independent Gazetteer*, November 30, 1787. (Pages 39-45)

1.   The rebellion in Massachusetts, now known as Shays's Rebellion, which began in August 1786, was used to justify the writing of the new Constitution and to argue for the necessity of approving it rapidly.

Notes

Centinel No. 5—Published in *The Independent Gazetteer*, December 4, 1787. (Pages 46-51)

Centinel No. 6—Published in *The Independent Gazetteer*, December 26, 1787. (Pages 52-55)

Centinel No. 7—Published in *The Independent Gazetteer*, December 29, 1787. (Pages 56-57)

Centinel No. 8—Published in *The Independent Gazetteer*, January 2, 1788. (Pages 58-62)

Centinel No. 9—Published in *The Independent Gazetteer*, January 8, 1788. (Pages 63-66)

1. Centinel here reminds his fellow citizens of the part that local and state politics then played in what we would now call national politics. His focus on the local shows his integrity—a willingness to use the means that were in keeping with his desired ends. When he attempts to go beyond the local, he calls for the formation of committees of correspondence, the means used prior to and during the Revolution.

2. Centinel here puts a paraphrase of a famous speech from Shakespeare's *The Tempest* to political use.

3. Centinel's almost obsessional concern about interference with the dissemination of information and debate shows his realization that the freedom of the press is useless without the freedom to circulate what issues from the press.

Centinel No. 10—Published in *The Independent Gazetteer*, January 12, 1788. (Pages 67-69)

1. James Wilson

2. Robert Morris (January 31, 1734-May 8, 1806) is best remembered as "the financier of the American Revolution." Centinel provides grounds for doubting the legitimacy of the title —or, rather, for finding irony in it: the Revolution financed him. Washington stayed in Morris's home during the Convention.

3. Gouverneur Morris (January 31, 1752-November 6, 1816) was a delegate from Pennsylvania to the Convention of 1787 although he had been born into the "landed aristocracy" of New York state. Washington appointed him minister to France in 1792. Many of

his widespread business interests were joint ventures with Robert Morris.

Centinel No. 11—Published in *The Independent Gazetteer*, January 16, 1788. (Pages 70-73)

1. Luther Martin (1748?-July 10, 1826) was a delegate from Maryland to the Convention of 1787, actively opposed a strong central government there, and walked out of the Convention without signing the Constitution. Henry Adams described Martin as "drunken, generous, slovenly, grand," and as "a bull-dog of federalism."

2. The authors of *The Federalist Papers*—Hamilton, Madison, and Jay.

3. Henry Home, Lord Kames (1696-1782), was a Scottish judge and a writer on a wide range of subjects, praised by Boswell and mocked by Dr. Johnson.

Centinel No. 12—Published in *The Independent Gazetteer*, January 23, 1788. (Pages 74-77)

1. William Findley (1741?-April 5, 1821) was, like George Bryan, Samuel's father, an Irish-born Presbyterian. He was identified with the "Whiskey Rebellion" of 1794 and wrote a *History of the Insurrection in the Four Western Counties of Pennsylvania* (1796).

Centinel No. 13—Published in *The Independent Gazetteer*, January 30, 1788. (Pages 78-81)

1. The interference with public debate continues to haunt Centinel.

2. Dr. Benjamin Rush (December 24, 1745-April 19, 1813), best remembered as a physician, wrote in favor of the Constitution in 1787 and served with James Wilson in the Pennsylvania ratifying convention. He and Wilson also led the campaign for the Pennsylvania Constitution of 1789. Rush was appointed treasurer of the United States mint by Federalist president John Adams.

3. James Wilson

Centinel No. 14—Published in *The Independent Gazetteer*, February 5, 1788. (Pages 82-89)

Notes

Centinel No. 15—Published in *The Independent Gazetteer*, February 22, 1788. (Pages 90-91)

1. The reference is to Shays's Rebellion.

Centinel No. 16—Published in *The Independent Gazetteer*, February 26, 1788. (Pages 92-94)

1. James Wilson

2. Robert Morris

3. The original quotes Article VI in a footnote: "The senators and representatives before mentioned and the members of the several state legislatures, and all executive and judicial officers, both of the United States and of the several states, shall be bound by oath to support this constitution." Centinel then says: "Were ever public defaulters so effectively screened! Not only the administrators of the general government, but also of the state governments, are prevented by oath from doing justice to the public; and the legislature of Pennsylvania could not without perjury insist upon the delinquent states discharging their arrears."

Centinel No. 17—Published in *The Independent Gazetteer*, March 24, 1788. (Pages 95-97)

1. Robert Morris

2. Willing and Morris

3. Thomas Mifflin (January 10, 1744-January 20, 1800) was a delegate from Pennsylvania to the Convention of 1787 but took little part in the debates.

4. Francis Hopkinson (October 2, 1734-May 9, 1791), a musician and artist as well as a writer, he supported ratification of the Constitution. He was named director of the "Grand Federal procession," one of the circuses staged in Philadelphia to celebrate Pennsylvania's ratification of the Constitution. Washington appointed him a judge of the United States court of the eastern district of Pennsylvania.

Centinel No. 18—Published in *The Independent Gazetteer*, April 9, 1788. (Pages 98-103)

1. The intercepted letters referred to here appear to have been by George Bryan.

2. Samuel Bryan has been credited with the authorship of this document.

3. Here Centinel explicitly draws attention to the influence of Shays's Rebellion on the Constitution.

4. Part of Centinel's aim was to firmly establish the free flow of information and discussion.

5. Samuel Bryan uses this opportunity to at once deny that his father is the author of Centinel's letters and to publicly praise his father. There is no doubt that Samuel Bryan learned his politics at his father's knee and that their views were virtually identical.

Centinel No. 19—Published in *The Independent Gazetteer*, October 7, 1788. (Pages 104-106)

Centinel No. 20—Published in *The Independent Gazetteer*, November 13, 1788. (Pages 107-111)

1. Dr. Benjamin Rush

2. Centinel inserted the following as a footnote here in the original "It is astonishing to think how successful this artifice has been. The disaffected were too highly prejudiced against the constitutional Whigs by the odious light in which they were continually represented by the well-born and their minions, as they were brought to consider them as the most violent, unprincipled, and abandoned of men, who were conspiring against the lives, property, and happiness of all other classes of people. Under such impressions two very worthy quakers, Robert Smith and Jonathan Morris, were, after the repeal of the test-law, elected members of the legislature for Chester county. But what was the astonishment of these honest men, when, in pursuing the dictates of their conscience and judgement, they found that in almost every vote they harmonized with the constitutionalists, and differed with those men they had been so highly prejudiced in favor of, whose corrupt principles and views they had now a demonstration of. Often have I heard them express their ardent wish, that all those of their constituents who were under the same delusion that they had been, might have the same opportunity of seeing, and judging themselves. But the upright conduct of these men was so highly displeasing to the junto, that at the next election they were

turned out. Indeed, during the course of the year that they were in the assembly, they were continually warned of the consequences of daring to exercise their judgement, and voting against the measures of the well-born; but they virtuously answered that they would not purchase a seat in the legislature at the expense of their integrity and the duty they owed their country."

3. Here is another quirk of history that suggests humanity is moving backwards. It is perhaps wishful thinking that those who concern themselves with Irish politics now will reach the clarity of Centinel soon.

4. Joseph Reed (1741-1785) was adjutant general of the Continental Army and served as president of the supreme executive council of Pennsylvania from 1778 to 1781.

Centinel No. 21—Published in *The Independent Gazetteer*, November 8, 1788. (Pages 112-115)

1. Centinel's immediate sympathy with the revolutionary movement in France and his recognition that the movement had been inspired by the example of the United States help to establish another difference between him and the Federalists: the Federalists were quick to reestablish ties with England and remained anti-French almost to a man.

Centinel No. 22—Published in *The Independent Gazetteer*, November 14, 1788. (Pages 116-122)

1. Dr. Benjamin Rush

2. Robert Morris

3. Centinel here is no doubt thinking of his own experience and, more, that of his father.

Centinel No. 23—Published in *The Independent Gazetteer*, November 20, 1788. (Pages 123-127)

Centinel No. 24—Published in *The Independent Gazetteer*, November 24, 1788. (Pages 128-130)

Selected Bibliography

John B. McMaster and Frederick D. Stone, *Pennsylvania and the Federal Constitution, 1787-1788* (Philadelphia, 1888)

Burton Alva Konkle, *George Bryan and the Constitution of Pennsylvania, 1731-1791* (Philadelphia, 1922)

Jackson Turner Main, *The Antifederalists: Critics of the Constitution 1781-1788* (Chapel Hill, 1961)

Saul Cornell, "Reflections on 'The Late Remarkable Revolution in Government': Aedanus Burke and Samuel Bryan's Unpublished History of the Ratification of the Federal Constitution," *The Pennsylvania Magazine of History & Biography*, Vol. CXII, No. 1 (January 1988)

Joseph S. Foster, *In Pursuit of Equal Liberty: George Bryan and the Revolution in Pennsylvania* (The Pennsylvania State University Press, 1994)

Index

Adams, John, 8

Anarchy, preferable to despotism, 70

Antifederalist writers of New York, 65

Aristocracy, permanent, as the aim of the United States Constitution, 14

Articles of confederation, inadequacy of, 3-4, 39

necessary expansion of powers of Congress under, 42

Beard, Charles, 1

Bill of Rights, and the Pennsylvania Constitution, 6

reasons for absence of from U.S. Constitution, 17

Blackstone, 23

"Brutus," pen name of Robert Yates, 38, 65

Bryan, George, 3

Burke, Aedanus, 4

Centinel, on use of pen name by, 103

Charles the First, fate of as potential fate of Federalists, 56

Checks and balances, critique of, 8-9

Clymer, George, 130

Colden, governor of New York, 24

Commerce, need for regulation of as reason for Constitutional Convention, 42

Common Sense, by Thomas Paine, 97

"Conciliator," James Wilson as, 27

Congress, expansion of powers of under Articles of Confederation, 42

method of forwarding proposed Constitution to the states by, 30

Conspiracy, the Constitution as a result of, 31

Conspirators, as appropriate description of Federalists, 74

Constitution, adoption of by Massachusetts, 90-91

as the result of a conspiracy, 31

Constitutional convention, authority of, 33

need for regulation of commerce as reason for, 42

secrecy of, 17

Constitutionalists, political party in Pennsylvania, 118

Cromwell, Oliver, 54

Despotism, as worst of all possible evils, 15

Dickinson, John, 18

Digby, George, Earl of Bristol, 55

Dunlap and Claypoole, printers, 38

Federal Gazette, 116

The Federalist Papers, 2, 72

Findley, William, 76

Fitzsimons, Thomas, 130

Forms of government, no proof of reality, 20

France, political situation in, 112-113

Franklin, Benjamin, 128

Free or republican government, conditions for, 9

"A Freeman," James Wilson as, 79

Government, purposes of, 7

141

Index

Index

FIFTH SEASON PRESS is dedicated to publishing works of literary or historical interest that might otherwise remain unavailable—the lost, the forgotten, and the untranslated. Other current and forthcoming titles include:

Chatterton by Ernest Lacy
ISBN 1-892355-00-0
This one-act tragedy in blank verse by a forgotten American poet and playwright moved audiences from coast to coast in the 1890s when actress Julia Marlowe performed the title role. A dramatic examination of what might best be called the political economy of genius, the play is here supplemented with an Introduction and Commentary by Michele Mollo and a number of illustrations, including a reproduction of an etching of Julia Marlowe playing the part of Thomas Chatterton, the Romantic poet.

The Right to be Lazy by Paul Lafargue
Written by a son-in-law of Karl Marx, this is the wittiest polemic to emerge from the international socialist movement of the nineteenth century. The new translation by Len Bracken highlights both the relevance and irrelevance of Lafargue's thought for contemporary society.

For more information write:
Fifth Season Press
P.O. Box 204
Ardmore, PA 19003